Contents

Part 1 Everyware, everywear, everywhere

You can find this part of the block online. A link is provided on the TU100 website.

Part 2 Cloud computing

You can find this part of the block online. A link is provided on the TU100 website.

Part 3 Location, location, location

You can find this part of the block online. A link is provided on the TU100 website.

Part 4 Glue

The Open University

TU100
My digital life

Block 3

My place

This publication forms part of the Open University module TU100 *My digital life*. Details of this and other Open University modules can be obtained from the Student Registration and Enquiry Service, The Open University, PO Box 197, Milton Keynes MK7 6BJ, United Kingdom (tel. +44 (0)845 300 60 90; email general-enquiries@open.ac.uk).

Alternatively, you may visit the Open University website at www.open.ac.uk where you can learn more about the wide range of modules and packs offered at all levels by The Open University.

To purchase a selection of Open University materials visit www.ouw.co.uk, or contact Open University Worldwide, Walton Hall, Milton Keynes MK7 6AA, United Kingdom for a brochure (tel. +44 (0)1908 858793; fax +44 (0)1908 858787; email ouw-customer-services@open.ac.uk).

The Open University
Walton Hall, Milton Keynes
MK7 6AA

First published 2011. [Second edition 2014.]

Edited and designed by The Open University.

Typeset by SR Nova Pvt. Ltd, Bangalore, India.

Printed in the United Kingdom by Latimer Trend and Company Ltd, Plymouth.

ISBN 978 1 7800 7921 9

2.1

Part 5 Giving it all away

Part 1

Everyware, everywear, everywhere

Authors: Christine Gardner and Elaine Thomas

You can find this part of the block online. A link is provided on the TU100 website.

Part 2

Cloud computing

Author: John Woodthorpe

You can find this part of the block online. A link is provided on the TU100 website.

Part 3

Location, location, location

Author: Arosha Bandara

You can find this part of the block online. A link is provided on the TU100 website.

Part 4

Glue

Author: Mike Richards

Introduction

So far in this module you have learned a great deal about data – how it is created, manipulated, transported and stored. This part of TU100 is concerned with the value of data and how it can be protected. Data is the glue that holds our society together; when it is lost we lose important relationships, knowledge and our past.

We are in the midst of a momentous cultural and technological revolution. Previously our records were written on relatively durable, age-old materials such as paper or canvas, or etched into stone and metal. But now, an increasing amount of data representing our lives – from music, art and writing, to tax returns and health records – is ceasing to exist as a physical item and only ever takes the form of strings of zeroes and ones. Data can be considered as having a life of its own from the moment it is created through to the time when it is finally deleted. The life of a piece of data is often perilous – it can be misfiled and lost, be accidentally deleted or simply succumb to the ravages of time. Sometimes data is created and destroyed in the blink of an eye; at other times it might resurface, often without warning and with unpredictable consequences. Conversely, data can be almost immortal when it is copied. No matter how many copies are destroyed, there is a chance that some of the data will still survive.

During this part you will see how it is necessary to start considering data as a valuable entity, every bit as important as the physical infrastructure of our houses, cars and great artworks. And just as we protect our material assets with repairs, insurance and physical locks, we must equally start to protect our largely intangible digital data. Our data must be protected, not only when it is actively being created and used, but also as a valuable historical record. If we mishandle or neglect digital data, we are faced with the very real prospect that large parts of our modern civilisation will fail to leave a historical record and many of our achievements will be lost forever. There is even a term for this prospect – a *Digital Dark Age*.

Historians once used the term 'Dark Ages' to describe more than 900 years of European civilisation between the collapse of the Western Roman Empire in the fifth century and the beginning of the Italian Renaissance in the fifteenth century. These historians felt that the crumbling of Rome's authority marked the beginning of a relative decline in European culture that was characterised by limited artistic and scientific achievements and grinding poverty. In fact, more recent research shows that the European 'Dark Ages' experienced any number of cultural flowerings: the Dark Ages only appear to be 'dark' today because many contemporary records were lost in much later wars, genocides and social revolutions.

Similarly the new Dark Age, if it occurs, will not be caused by any decline in our civilisation; rather it will be caused by digital data becoming unreadable, either through changes in technology or by the physical deterioration of the medium holding that data.

We are now scrambling to find solutions to a host of problems raised in our headlong rush towards digital technologies; fortunately we can draw on a multitude of historical cases to devise strategies for preserving digital information in a meaningful manner.

Activity 1 (exploratory)

Write a sentence or two to explain what is meant by the phrase 'Digital Dark Age'.

Comment

The phrase 'Digital Dark Age' refers to a situation in which digital data becomes unreadable, either through changes in technology or by the physical deterioration of the medium holding the data. Important information about our lives, relationships and culture would then be lost.

Learning outcomes

Your study of this part will help you to do the following.

Knowledge and understanding

- Explain the importance of developing methods of preserving data.
- Describe how operating systems manage data.
- Describe how computer data can be protected in the event of a criminal or civil investigation.
- Describe how standards are developed.
- Explain the role of emulation in preserving computer data.

Cognitive skills

- Give examples of data recovery from historical sources.
- Discuss the role of standards in technology.
- Decide on an appropriate strategy for backing up computer data.
- Discuss the value of the long-term persistence of data.

Key skills

- Write a short report on a technical subject after completing independent research.
- Perform statistical analysis to identify trends in data.

1

How long does data last?

The survival of any piece of data is limited by a number of factors. The most obvious of these is that an individual piece of data cannot outlast the lifetime of the medium on which it is stored. However, even if data remains intact it is possible that we will lose the ability to read it.

1.1   Two Domesdays – how to (and how not to) keep data

The first Domesday

William I of England was not a popular monarch. Following his victory at Hastings in 1066, William set about turning England into a vassal of his native Normandy. Government was centralised around the court, and taxes flowed straight to the king. In 1086 William ordered an unprecedented survey of the entirety of England in order to establish the taxable value and resources of every settlement, and from that to establish what was owed to the Crown.

> Then he [King William] sent his men over all England into every shire and had them find out how many 100 hides there were in the shire, or what land and cattle the King himself had in the country or what dues he ought to have in the 12 months from the shire. He also recorded how much land his archbishops had and his bishops and his abbots and his earls how much each man who was a landholder in England had in land or livestock and how much money it was worth.
>
> Extract from the Anglo-Saxon Chronicle, MS Laud Misc. 636, fol. 62v, The Bodleian Library, University of Oxford

Such were the overreaching powers of the process that William's subjects directly compared it to the inevitable and terrible divine judgement in the Book of Revelation and called the survey 'the book of reckoning' – 'the Domesday Book'.

Domesday comes from the Old English word *dom*, which can be translated as either 'reckoning' or 'judgement' and is the root of the modern English word 'doom'. William's survey is often incorrectly called 'The Doomsday Book'.

The result was not just one, but two colossal volumes (see Figure 1). The first, called the Little Domesday, may have been a trial survey. It is a highly detailed survey of what are now Essex, Suffolk and Norfolk, right down to the numbers of livestock held on each farm. The Great Domesday contains the remainder of England with the exception of the far north of England and certain towns (amongst others, London and Bristol were not surveyed), in much less exhaustive detail.

Figure 1   The Domesday Book in the National Archives: the two topmost books are the Great Domesday, while the Little Domesday is bound into the three lower books (the covers are modern rebindings)

Between them, the two Domesdays contain some 13 418 place names and assessed the income of England to be £73 000 per year. This figure may seem extraordinarily low to a modern reader, but it is worth remembering that a noble of 1086 might only have earned a few tens of pounds each year. The books provide an unparalleled insight into Norman England – it is possible to use them to discover towns that have long since vanished, how many slaves existed in England, the professions practised, military conscription records, the changes in ownership of land between the Norman invasion and the time of the survey, and the relative rates of prosperity around the country.

Figure 2 shows the first page of the Domesday survey of Wiltshire. The table on the left-hand side is a numbered list of the county's landholders, while the text on the right is the beginning of the description of the lands in the county. It begins with the king's holdings called 'Terra Regis'; later pages list lands belonging to bishops and then other nobles. The red lines through text are not deletions – rather, they are an early way of highlighting important material such as place names. On this page, the scribe ran out of room; rather than starting on a fresh page, he added the smaller text at the very foot of the document.

We don't know the exact date that the Domesday Book was completed: it may have been finished as late as 1090, but even so that is a remarkable achievement given the limitations of technology and communications in eleventh-century England. Over the next two centuries, a number of copies of the Domesday Book were made for government work, including one for the Exchequer (the forerunner of the modern Treasury). The first 'public' copy was completed between 1767 and 1800, and was followed in

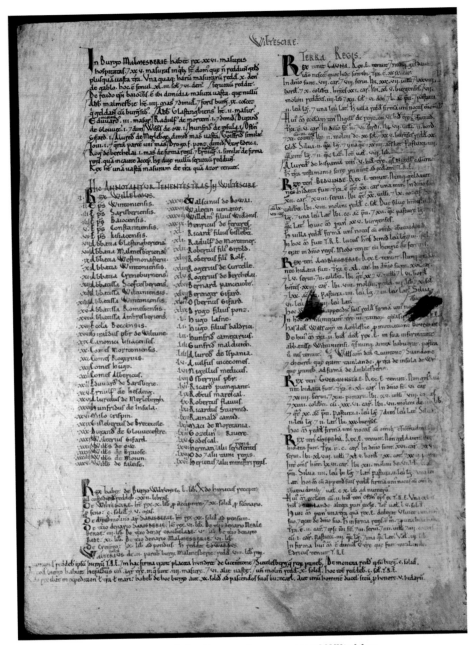

Figure 2 The first page of the Domesday survey of Wiltshire

1861 by a photographic reproduction of the entire book intended for libraries. The general public have been able to buy relatively inexpensive versions of the books for more than a hundred years. In addition, recently much of the Domesday Book has been made available on the internet. The original volumes are now located in the National Archives at Kew in London. Because of their inestimable value and great age, they are preserved behind glass and cannot be handled by members of the public.

The Domesday Book survives in part because of the way it was written and then stored. It was handwritten in Latin on parchment (see Box 1) bound into volumes. The document was mainly written using permanent black ink made from oak galls, which has gradually turned brown with age but remains legible. Highlights were written in a red ink containing lead oxide that has retained its brilliant colour. The two volumes remained in the possession of the Crown from the eleventh to the nineteenth century, carefully protected in a specially commissioned wooden chest. The books were rarely removed from this chest except when legal cases needed to refer to the original documents.

Many cases concerning property law in medieval England were only resolved by reference to the Domesday Book. It was considered so important that as late as the thirteenth century, scribes copied the document precisely – even so far as including deleted text and corrections.

Box 1 Parchment

Parchment is made from the skins of sheep, goats or calves (though in the latter case it is called vellum). The skins are soaked in an alkaline solution, then stretched and dried. Parchment was the main material used in books until the introduction of printing in the fifteenth century. It is relatively tough and durable, and provides an excellent surface for writing.

Parchment is still used for important legal documents (such as Acts of Parliament), the Jewish Torah and commemorative publications.

Activity 2 (self-assessment)

Why has the original Domesday Book survived, and why can it be used and understood many centuries after it was written?

800 years later ...

In 1984 over one million Britons, many of them children, began to collect information about their communities. They wrote essays about the geography and history of their area as well as describing their everyday lives. This information was being collected by a consortium consisting of the BBC, The Open University, Acorn Computers (who manufactured the immensely popular BBC microcomputers), the European Union, the software company Logica and the Dutch electronics giant Philips. Information from the public was combined with cutting-edge computer graphics, professional video and data taken from the then-current 1981 national census to produce one of the first recognisable multimedia products: the BBC Domesday Project, released in 1986.

BBC Domesday was designed to work with the BBC Master microcomputer found in many British schools. As you saw in Block 1

Part 2, the BBC Micros were originally developed in the early 1980s for the BBC Computer Literacy Project and became extremely popular in schools because of their rugged design, excellent (for the time) programming language and large variety of educational software titles. The BBC Master was the final version of the BBC Micro, containing 128 KB of RAM.

The Domesday data itself required a novel storage solution. The most common technologies of the day were floppy disks and cassette tapes, both of which were hopelessly inadequate for the volume of data being collected – the standard BBC Micro floppy disk held just 100 KB! And not only were hard disks far too expensive for most schools, even the largest supported by the BBC computers could store only 20 MB of data. So instead, the consortium chose to store the Domesday Project on a pair of Philips Laservision discs, each capable of storing 600 MB on 30 cm double-sided optical discs.

Laservision (later rebranded as Laserdisc) was an ancestor of CDs and DVDs that stored analogue information on an optical disc. The most common use for this technology was for home movies, as the discs offered far superior image quality to video tape.

As a result of these decisions, anyone wishing to use the Domesday Project needed to have a BBC Master microcomputer expanded with a second microprocessor and a network card, and then buy a specially modified Philips LV-ROM Laservision player – the aptly named 'Domesday Player'. The cost of a single computer, an optical drive and a set of discs was £4000, a colossal amount of money for most schools. Eventually prices fell, but even so, the Domesday Player did not sell in the expected numbers and was a commercial failure.

Despite this, the Domesday Project at first appeared to be an enormous success. It was the first time many people had seen the potential of multimedia technologies: this was one of the first mass-collaboration projects ever undertaken, providing an incredibly detailed snapshot of British society between 1984 and 1986. However, then catastrophe struck. Within a few years of publication, the whole project had become practically inaccessible. There were a number of reasons for this:

- The BBC microcomputers had become obsolescent. Their replacement, the Acorn Archimedes, never achieved mainstream success as schools rapidly standardised around IBM PC-compatible computers.

- Laserdisc, which had been expected to replace video tape for entertainment purposes, remained a minority format – as well as being big and expensive, the discs could not be used to record programmes, unlike the much cheaper video tape. Philips discontinued production of Domesday-compatible players and components.

- The Domesday Project had been programmed in such a way that it was extremely difficult to modify the software for use on, i.e. *port* to, other computer platforms.

A further concern surrounded the optical discs themselves. Each Laserdisc stored data much like a modern DVD, using a thin, highly reflective aluminium layer protected by a polycarbonate plastic platter. Two platters, glued back to back, produced one double-sided Laserdisc. Philips had expected this tough plastic media would survive many decades of everyday use, but by the middle of the 1990s it became clear that these claims might be extremely optimistic. People who had bought films on Laserdisc were reporting that their once pristine pictures were progressively deteriorating to the point where some discs were no longer playable. The phenomenon became known as 'laser rot', and was soon found to be caused by atmospheric oxygen penetrating poorly glued discs and attacking the reflective data layer, where it gradually turned silver aluminium into transparent aluminium oxide that could not be read by laser light.

'Laser rot' also affected some early DVDs, especially the double-sided 'flipper' discs that were made by gluing two single-sided discs back to back. The phenomenon has largely disappeared with the transition to single-sided 'dual layer' discs, and with better manufacturing technologies.

1.2   Obsolescence

The BBC Domesday Project is an example of two forms of obsolescence.

- *Technological obsolescence* is the process by which an existing technology is replaced by a newer one. Some examples include the replacement of the telegraph by the telephone, the end of horse-drawn transport and the transition to digital television.

- *Digital obsolescence* is a type of technological obsolescence in which digital data is rendered inaccessible by changes in computer technologies. It can be caused by changes to hardware or software. Some examples of technologies ended by digital obsolescence include the floppy disk and the mainframe computers of the 1960s.

Our modern world is dominated by the rapid turnover of technologies, driven in part by technological development and in part by the demands of a consumer society. The rate of change appears to be accelerating, with technologies being replaced at an ever-increasing pace.

Some new technologies offer *backwards compatibility* with existing technologies – for example, DVD players offer backwards compatibility with CD players and can be used to play music, whilst Blu-ray players are backwards compatible with both DVD and CD.

In contrast, certain technologies are examples of *disruptive technology*; they require the user to adapt to their use, often by forcing them to buy new equipment. Despite this apparent drawback, disruptive technologies often end up dominating a market in which they offer substantial improvements or are much cheaper than previous technologies. An example of a disruptive technology is the digital camera, which is rapidly replacing film cameras in all but niche markets.

Activity 3 (exploratory)

Which of the following factors does *not* have a detrimental effect on the survival of data?

1   Disruptive technologies
2   Deterioration of storage media
3   Digital obsolescence
4   Backwards compatibility
5   Technological obsolescence

Comment

The answer is number 4. Backwards compatibility means that a new technology is compatible with existing ones, so it does not have a detrimental effect on the survival of data.

1.3   Conclusion

This session introduced you to the paradox that our modern technologies, which are capable of storing ever-increasing quantities and types of information, might actually be less accessible to future users than traditional technologies dating back thousands of years.

This session should have helped you with the following learning outcomes.

*   Explain the importance of developing methods of preserving data.
*   Give examples of data recovery from historical sources.

Preserving data

2

Session 1 demonstrated that data stored using modern technologies may not be as durable as data stored using traditional media. In this session you will see that it is possible to make some predictions of the behaviour of novel materials over an extended period of time.

Until the twentieth century, the best guarantee that information would be preserved was to carve it into a durable material such as stone or bone. The creators of Ancient Egyptian inscriptions and modern gravestones share a desire that their work will last forever. But how do modern materials compare with those available to the ancients, which we know last for thousands of years? We still use a few materials, such as paper, that would have been familiar to our predecessors, but many commonplace media were only invented in the nineteenth or twentieth century and we have little evidence of their durability.

2.1   Everything has a lifetime

Inevitably, the medium holding any data will deteriorate until it becomes unusable. Linen and canvas rot; even stone crumbles given sufficient time. Some processes take centuries, whilst others happen remarkably quickly; a newspaper left on a bright windowsill will turn yellow and begin to crisp in a few months. The chances are that if you examine the edges of your treasured books, you will see the same yellow discoloration that is found on old newspapers. Paper is one of the most common ways of storing data, and its deterioration is a pressing problem for archivists and librarians. The chemical processes that allowed the industrial manufacture of paper in the nineteenth and twentieth centuries have produced a material with a shorter lifespan than that of handmade paper from previous centuries. A great deal of effort is now going into finding ways of preserving important documents before they become unusable, as well as making better paper and ink.

We can make accurate lifespan predictions for conventional materials such as paper because archivists and librarians have accumulated experience in handling books and other paper documents. Organisations such as the British Library provide guidelines aimed at preserving paper for as long as possible, and we can be confident that documents printed on expensive archival paper will last for several centuries. Calculating the lifespan of computer storage media, however, is more problematic, since many of the materials used in their construction are synthetic and of recent invention.

Activity 4 (self-assessment)

Spend a few minutes listing some types of storage media used by computers or other digital devices.

Of all the types of media I mentioned in my answer to the previous activity, magnetic storage has the longest history, going back to the nineteenth century. Tape is the oldest recognisable magnetic storage: it began around 1930 with the splendidly named Blattnerphone. However, the knowledge that magnetic recording was *possible* more than eighty years ago does not answer the question of whether those recordings are still *usable*.

With no history to rely on, it is necessary to make predictions of how materials will behave over prolonged periods. A well-established rule of chemistry is that the rate at which substances degrade increases in a predictable way when they are exposed to higher temperatures, higher humidity levels, greater concentrations and increased amounts of ultraviolet light (such as that from the sun). *Accelerated ageing* is a technique for testing the lifespan of novel materials or objects that attempts to compress many years of such exposure into a relatively short period of time. The object to be tested is brought to a laboratory and exposed to far greater levels of potentially damaging substances than would be found in real life; so the object might be baked, exposed to pure oxygen or bombarded with intense ultraviolet light. After a period, the object will be removed and compared to an identical sample that has not been aged. Any changes are measured and a predicted lifetime established.

Ageing gives only a guideline lifespan for any product. The real lifespan of the object is dependent on how it is used, how much it is used and how it is cared for. In most cases the *actual* lifespan of an object is much less than that predicted by ageing techniques. Some expected lifespans for common computer storage media are given in Table 1, which was compiled by ZDNet (2002) in association with computer manufacturers and technology experts. The findings might surprise you when you consider that low-technology storage in the form of paper can last for centuries.

Table 1 Lifespans of some computer storage media

Medium	Example	Lifespan (years)
Hard disks	Computer hard disk	3–6
Magnetic tape	Computer data backup	10–20
Magnetic disks	Floppy disk	1–5
Optical discs	DVD	10–100
Static memory	Digital camera memory card	50–100

Even within these figures, there is a wide disparity between the best-performing products and those that will degrade the quickest. A 2006 study conducted by the United States National Institute of Standards and Technology (NIST) revealed that while recordable DVDs *should* be usable for more than 100 years, less than half of the discs tested *could* be expected to be readable after just 15 years (The X Lab, n.d.). The study also showed that there was a wide range in the quality of discs from different manufacturers; the worst-performing recordable DVDs could be expected to show appreciable deterioration in less than two years.

2.2 Conclusion

The only reasonable conclusion to the discussion in this session is that no known data storage technology will last indefinitely. Rather, media have a limited lifetime before they degrade beyond use, and that lifetime may not actually be known. We need to back up our data.

This session should have helped you with the following learning outcome.

- Explain the importance of developing methods of preserving data.

3

Backing up data

So far you have seen that data itself can be remarkably resilient; its lifetime is largely limited by the medium on which it is stored. Paper rots, magnetic disks gradually lose their coatings and even optical discs are consumed by the air. Long-term threats to our data are serious enough, but we must also consider everyday threats including:

- accidentally deleting a file or program
- losing disks, computers or memory cards
- hardware failures such as a hard disk crash
- software bugs that prevent data being written to a storage device or cause it to be corrupted as it is written
- disasters such as fire or flooding
- crimes including terrorism, theft and acts of sabotage such as hacking.

Activity 5 (self-assessment)

Look at the list of risks to data above. Do you think any of them apply to you and your computer?

There are serious consequences of losing data, which can be expressed as a series of costs:

1   The cost of recreating the lost data – either by buying new hardware and software or by re-entering the lost data (which may not always be possible).
2   The cost of continuing without the lost data.
3   The cost of informing others about the loss.

These costs cannot just be expressed in terms of money. For instance, the last cost – of informing others – is not just limited to postage and email charges; a company that suffers a data loss can also suffer a loss in its reputation as a professional organisation. This problem is greatly magnified if personal data has been lost. For instance, at the end of 2008 the blog provider JournalSpace went into liquidation after the crucial database containing its customers' blogs was corrupted by a disgruntled former employee. This criminal action should not have proved fatal, but it became clear that the six-year-old company had not been keeping complete *backups* of its data. JournalSpace customers were able to recover some of their data using copies of their postings held in Google's giant cache, but JournalSpace's reputation was ruined. JournalSpace was later reborn under new management, but by then it had lost most of its users.

The risk of data loss cannot be completely eliminated, but it can be minimised. One of the most important ways of minimising the effect of any loss is by backing up data – making secure copies of it to a separate device, to a separate disk or even to a different location. The only way of guaranteeing that data will remain useful in the future is to regularly copy (*migrate*) it from one medium to another and to make multiple copies.

Activity 6 (self-assessment)

Why should we migrate data regularly, and why should we make more than one copy?

3.1 Types of backup

The simplest way to back up the data on your computer is to make regular *complete backups* – copies of every file on the disk. However, as you can imagine, backing up data in this manner requires huge amounts of storage space and takes a great deal of time. For this reason, two other types of backup are common.

1 *Incremental backups* save time and storage space by copying only those files that have been created or altered since the previous backup. The first backup is indistinguishable from a complete backup – every file on the disk is copied. Subsequent backups store only changes to the disk's content (such as new files, modified files and deleted data) that have occurred since the previous backup. Incremental backups allow for fast, regular backups that do not consume too much space, and so they are the most common form of data backup. However, the serious drawback to incremental backups is that the loss of *any* single backup file will result in serious data loss.

2 *Differential backups* offer some of the time- and space-saving benefits of incremental backups as well as greater levels of security. Once again, the first backup copies every file on the disk. Subsequent backups copy every file on the disk that has changed since the original backup. In this case, the loss of any but the original backup is less important since data is stored in more than one backup file. However, differential backups are less secure than complete backups since the loss of the original backup will still cause serious data loss.

Users who adopt either incremental or differential backups are also advised to take regular complete backups of their data to protect against the failure of the original backups. It is vital that backups are kept in a secure location, especially when they might contain personal or valuable data.

Activity 7 (exploratory)

Arrange complete, incremental and differential backups first in order of their security and then in order of the amount of space they require. If you have difficulty with this activity then a set of short animations demonstrating the differences between the three types of backup is available in the resources page associated with this part on the TU100 website.

Comment

Security

From most secure to least secure: complete backup, differential backup, incremental backup.

Storage space

From least space to most space: incremental backup, differential backup, complete backup.

Archiving data

In a perfect world each of us would keep a backup of every piece of data we ever use, but it is simply impractical for most of us to buy ever more media to store our backups. Instead most media are reused after a certain period of time, with old backups being written over by new data. Businesses in particular must retain backups for a number of years (for legal and tax purposes) before media can be recycled.

Important files, especially those of historic or legal interest, should be archived so that they are never overwritten. In many countries it is a legal obligation for companies to archive data for auditing purposes. Governments around the world are recognising the importance of archiving data and authorising national bodies to store important digital records. In the UK, this work is managed by the Public Records Office and the British Library.

A failure to keep proper *archives* caused great embarrassment for the White House in the USA. The Presidential Records Act (PRA) requires the presidency to retain all communications so that they can be used by future historians. During 2007 it became clear that the White House had not been retaining email traffic and might have violated the PRA. The issue was made public when a Senate investigation into possible political interference in the dismissal of US attorneys requested emails from the then Bush administration. The White House conceded that around fifty members of staff had been conducting government business using computers, mobile phones and email accounts provided by the Republican Party for campaigning purposes. Until 2004, the email servers belonging to the Republican Party had automatically deleted all emails after thirty days, and some of the staff had the ability to delete emails from the system. US law prohibits political campaigning in government offices, and the staff should have been using the fully backed-up White House system. An out-of-court settlement was reached between the White House and campaigners in late 2009. Some 22 million emails were eventually recovered and sent for archiving under the PRA. At the time of writing, the White House was still attempting to recover a further 5 million more missing emails.

3.2 Permanent storage technologies

Now that I have looked at issues of backups and archiving, I now want to turn to the different technologies that might be used to store the backed-up data.

Magnetic tape

Tape is an archaic computer storage technology that is still in widespread use. Film footage of computers from the 1950s and 1960s always showed long banks of reel-to-reel magnetic tape readers resembling old-fashioned tape recorders. In that period computer tape was used to hold programs and data as well as serving as a permanent store.

Computer (data) tapes are made from identical materials to those used in the more familiar audio cassettes and video tapes, but store their contents as digital rather than analogue values. The tape itself is made from thin plastic film coated in a magnetisable material such as iron or cobalt. The old-fashioned, but highly photogenic, reel-to-reel tapes (Figure 3a) have long since been replaced by tape cartridges, similar to video cassettes, that protect the fragile tape inside a robust plastic casing.

Technological advances allowed tape capacities to grow from 5 MB per tape in the mid-1960s to 1 terabyte (TB) at the time of writing (2010), whilst gradually reducing the size of the cartridge itself. Modern Ultrium tape cartridges are only 102 mm long, 105.4 mm wide and just 21.5 mm thick (Figure 3b).

Tape's huge capacity has meant that it is the only realistic backup choice for organisations generating huge amounts of data, whilst automated tape retrieval systems allow backups to be located rapidly, even in very large tape libraries (see Figure 4). However, digital magnetic tape has not been a popular medium for personal computer users and small businesses because the drives themselves are relatively expensive (although tape itself is relatively cheap). One exception was the very earliest microcomputers (especially in the UK), which often relied on much less robust and less reliable analogue cassette tapes for permanent data storage.

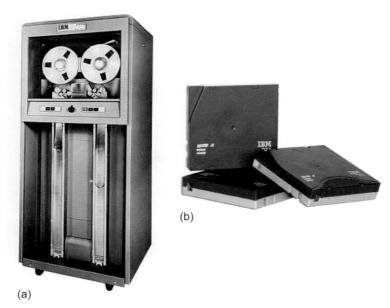

(b)

(a)

Figure 3 (a) The IBM 727, the very first tape drive, introduced in late 1953 – this machine stored data on open spools of magnetic tape and was used both as a backup device and for data storage, since it was much faster than the punch cards widely used at the time; (b) modern IBM LTO Ultrium tape cartridges, which are used by many modern computer backup systems

Figure 4 A robot operating in the tape library of the CERN nuclear physics research laboratory: when a backup is needed by a user, the robot locates and retrieves the relevant tape and loads it into a tape reader

The advantages and disadvantages of magnetic tape are as follows.

Advantages

1   Digital tape is extremely cheap per megabyte of storage and can store very large amounts of data. Tape is the most common method of permanently storing extremely large amounts of data such as those generated by scientific experiments. The LTO6 standard, which will be introduced in 2012, will store up to 3 TB on a single tape.

2   Tape cartridges are more resistant to damage than hard disks (although less robust than optical discs).

3   Tapes come in standard formats from a range of vendors. Even if one supplier fails, others are available.

4   Tape cartridges consume very little space in archives.

5   Tape can even be repaired if it snaps or tangles.

Disadvantages

1   Inexpensive hard disks offer greater capacities and speed for reading and writing data.

2   Digital tape is not widely supported in small offices or personal computer systems.

3   Digital tape is slow and inconvenient. It is a *linear access format*; which means that to find a file near the end of the tape it is necessary for the reader to traverse all of the tape up to that point (just like fast-forwarding a video tape) – on long tapes this can take a considerable amount of time.

4   High failure-rates of restores (high cost associated with this).

5   Encrypted storage is very hard to achieve.

Hard disks

Magnetic disks

The floppy disk has long since been superseded as a backup medium because of its limited capacity. Instead, hard disks offer an attractive medium.

Most PCs have sufficient internal space for a second hard disk that can be devoted to backups, or alternatively a relatively cheap external hard disk can be connected to a USB or FireWire port on a computer. More expensive disks can be connected directly to a network using Ethernet or Wi-Fi.

Magnetic disks are an example of a *random access format*. It is not necessary to spool backwards and forwards through the record to find a piece of data; instead, the reader can move directly to the record in question. As a result, disks are much faster than tape for both reading and writing data.

Activity 8 (exploratory)

Most computer operating systems allow users to 'partition' a hard disk so that it appears as more than one disk to the computer's operating system – so, for instance, a 2 TB hard disk could be partitioned into two 1 TB drives. It might be tempting to use one partition as a backup disk. Can you think why this might not be a good idea?

Comment

The reason this should not be done is that if the disk itself were to fail, the backup partition would no longer be accessible and you would lose all your data.

RAID

Conventionally, hard disk backups demanded very high-quality, highly reliable drives – and were correspondingly very expensive. In 1987, researchers at the University of Berkeley developed a way of making highly reliable backups on hard disks using much less expensive components. Their system is commonly known as a *Redundant Array of Inexpensive Disks (RAID)*, the name of which hints at its workings. Rather than storing data on a single disk, RAID writes each piece of data to an *array* of disks that appear as a single hard disk to the computer. The data is stored on more than one disk, so even if one were to fail, a copy of the data could be retrieved. There are a number of RAID configurations available, offering different levels of security.

Some manufacturers refer to RAID as a Redundant Array of *Independent* Disks, feeling that 'inexpensive' might mislead customers into thinking that RAID arrays are necessarily cheap.

Although RAID has yet to become a standard method of backing up for home users or small businesses, some computer manufacturers offer it as an option on personal computers or sell standalone RAID arrays. Other companies, such as Drobo, sell 'RAID-like' devices that can simply be plugged into a desktop computer using a USB or FireWire port. Figure 5 shows one such 'RAID-like' disk array: here the front of the unit has been opened, revealing hard disks in the top three slots and space for a fourth disk in the bottom slot.

Removable hard disks

Iomega's ZIP, JAZ and REV disks attempt to combine the familiarity and robustness of a floppy disk with the capacity of a hard disk. Disk drives such as the one shown in Figure 6 store data on robust plastic cartridges containing magnetic disks. The very earliest ZIP cartridges had a 100 MB capacity, whilst REV cartridges can contain up to 120 GB.

Whilst these devices offer an attractive alternative to optical discs or hard disks, they are reliant on a single vendor supplying both drives and cartridges. A similar technology from SyQuest Technologies was left an *orphan* in 1998 when that company went into liquidation. As supplies of drives, spare parts and cartridges dwindled, SyQuest users spent a great

Figure 5   A Data Robotics Drobo 'RAID-like' disk array: the three green lights show that the disks are working correctly, that data has been mirrored and that the unit has plenty of storage space, while the four blue lights at the bottom show that the Drobo is using only 40% of its maximum capacity

Figure 6   The Iomega REV disk drive, which can be used as a backup system for any computer with a USB port: up to 120 GB of data (or 240 GB if compression is used) can be stored on removable cartridges

deal of time and money migrating their data onto another format. In some cases, users lost data because their SyQuest drives failed before the data could be moved.

The advantages and disadvantages of hard disks (magnetic hard disks, RAID and removable hard disks) are as follows.

Advantages

1   Disks are relatively cheap and capacities are growing rapidly.
2   External hard disks can easily be moved between computers.
3   There are many disk manufacturers, all of whose products can be used in almost any computer.

4   There are a large number of backup programs designed to be used with hard disks. Many external disks are sold with applications to ease the backup process, or offer a 'one-touch' backup button.

Disadvantages

1   Hard disks are fragile and easily damaged if dropped or exposed to extremely high temperatures or magnetic fields.

2   Removable hard disks often rely on a single vendor whose long-term survival cannot be guaranteed.

3   If hard disks are used once to make a backup then archived, the replacement cost is much higher than for tape or optical media.

Solid-state disks (SSDs) and memory cards

Solid-state disks and memory cards store data in solid-state (i.e. silicon microchip) memory. At the time of writing, no manufacturer recommended these technologies for long-term backups because there are still considerable uncertainties over the lifespan of these relatively new devices. However, solid-state memory – especially the large, robust, compact flash cards used by cameras – appears to be extremely robust, with many reports of it surviving extreme conditions, even immersion in sea water.

The advantages and disadvantages of solid-state memory are as follows.

Advantages

1   Capacity is growing rapidly and prices are falling.

2   These devices are small, silent and extremely power-efficient because they have no moving parts – unlike other forms of storage.

3   Solid-state memory is mechanically reliable and physically robust to shock and environmental factors.

Disadvantages

1   The long-term reliability of these devices is largely unknown.

2   They are expensive when compared to other forms of storage.

3   They can be slow, especially when writing files to the disk.

Optical storage

The most common technology for optical storage is one of a number of competing writeable DVD standards including DVD-R, DVD+R, DVD-RW, DVD+RW and DVD-RAM. Most of these DVD formats can store 4.7 GB on a single disc, although so-called dual-layer discs and drives can store twice that. A newer, related technology, Blu-ray recordable (BD-R and BD-RE), can store up to 50 GB on each disc.

Some optical discs can only be written once. Others, whose names contain the letter 'W' or 'E', can be rewritten thousands of times – although not indefinitely.

The discs themselves are made by sandwiching a thin layer of metal or dye between two layers of transparent polycarbonate plastic. The metal or dye changes colour when exposed to red laser light. Digital data is written to the disc by pulsing a bright red laser light as the disc spins. When the laser is on, a tiny spot on the light-sensitive layer changes colour; when it is off, the layer remains intact. The data is read by reflecting a lower-powered beam from the light-sensitive layer. Bright and dark patches form a pattern of zeroes and ones that can be reconstructed into useful data.

The advantages and disadvantages of optical storage are as follows.

Advantages

1   Drives and media are extremely cheap and widespread. Most computers have an optical drive and the discs can be bought in supermarkets.

2   There are a large number of manufacturers, so there should be no problem with future supplies of discs.

3   More modern optical disc technologies (such as Blu-ray) also support most older types of disc such as DVD and CD.

4   The medium is relatively small – large amounts of data can be stored in a very small space.

5   The medium is robust. Discs can be posted and are able to survive regular use or being dropped. They are resistant to extremes of temperature and humidity, and immune to strong magnetic fields.

Disadvantages

1   Optical drives are relatively slow compared to hard disks, especially when writing data.

2   There are a large number of types of disc (especially recordable DVDs). Some of these types are not widely supported.

3   Their capacity is relatively low compared to hard disks. A 500 GB hard disk is relatively commonplace on modern computers; it would take more than 100 DVDs to make a complete backup of such a disk. Consequently, DVDs might be best suited to making backups of key data.

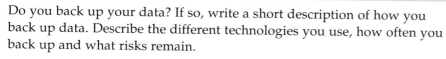

Activity 9 (exploratory)

Do you back up your data? If so, write a short description of how you back up data. Describe the different technologies you use, how often you back up and what risks remain.

If you don't perform backups, but you work for an organisation, briefly explain their backup procedure (you might need to talk to the person in charge of the company's computers).

If you do not perform backups and do not work for a company that does, briefly explain what sort of backup procedures would offer you a reasonable amount of security.

Comment

A video that describes The Open University's backup procedure may be found in the resources page associated with this part on the TU100 website.

3.3   Remote backups

Large businesses and organisations insure themselves even further against failure by storing backups away from their centre of operation. In the event of a disaster, there is a much greater likelihood that they can return to normal operations within a short period of time – after all, it is much easier to buy new computers than to recreate all of the records.

Offsite backups

Specialised companies offer specialised facilities where companies can hire storage space or machinery to hold backups. These offsite facilities might be nothing more than an extremely secure vault where tapes or disks can be deposited, but increasingly they are large server farms connected to very high-speed networks. Users can copy files to these servers as if they were part of their own network, the only bottleneck being the speed of the network between the offsite facility and the user.

The UK's largest such site is Telehouse UK in London's Docklands, which has partner sites in the USA and Japan. The London facility covers some 45 000 square metres and is used by over 700 large companies and internet service providers.

Backing up to the cloud

For many years, offsite backup was restricted to organisations who could afford relatively large monthly fees; however, cloud technology allows anyone to have offsite storage, and in many cases this storage is completely free. You learned about cloud backups in Part 2 of this block.

Once data is stored in the cloud, you can no longer be sure that it is entirely secure from prying eyes. Most companies have policies claiming that your data will be secure, but these cannot provide absolute insurance from attackers. You can guarantee that your data is safe in the cloud by using encryption to scramble the contents – you will learn more about using encryption in a later part.

Activity 10 (self-assessment)

JournalSpace, which you met earlier, used the RAID system to store its customers' data. However, RAID could not protect against the deliberate overwriting of that data. How could JournalSpace have better protected its customers' data?

Box 2 describes how backups succeeded in preserving the history of the internet itself.

Box 2 Backups saved the internet's history

Before the Web there was Usenet: an internet-wide discussion system divided into tens of thousands of threaded conferences whose topics covered every possible subject ranging from the dry and technical to the incredibly frivolous. Today, Usenet's text-only messages might seem hopelessly dated and limited, but from 1979 until the advent of the Web, it was the main way that internet users could share their interests with like-minded people. Some historic information was first posted on Usenet: it saw the first mention of MS-DOS and the Apple Mac, it was used by researchers to discuss their work on HIV and by engineers exploring the cause of the *Challenger* Space Shuttle disaster, and it was even used to announce a new technology called the World Wide Web.

Announcing the World Wide Web

On 6 August 1991, Tim Berners-Lee made a posting to Usenet announcing his work on the World Wide Web. The posting was sent to a group concerned with the development of hypertext systems hosted inside the 'alternative' hierarchy of Usenet – hence its name alt.hypertext. The posting is worth reading because you will recognise most of the attributes of the modern Web, although some of the terms we are familiar with (such as URL) hadn't yet been developed.

alt.hypertext
Message from discussion WorldWideWeb: Summary
Aug 6 1991, 8:37 pm

In article <6...@cernvax.cern.ch> I promised to post a short summary of the WorldWideWeb project. Mail me with any queries.

WorldWideWeb – Executive Summary

The WWW project merges the techniques of information retrieval and hypertext to make an easy but powerful global information system.

The project started with the philosophy that much academic information should be freely available to anyone. It aims to allow information sharing within internationally dispersed teams, and the dissemination of information by support groups.

Reader view

The WWW world consists of documents, and links. Indexes are special documents which, rather than being read, may be searched. The result of such a search is another ("virtual") document containing links to the documents found. A simple protocol ("HTTP") is used to allow a browser program to request a keyword search by a remote information server.

The web contains documents in many formats. Those documents which are hypertext, (real or virtual) contain links to other documents, or places within documents. All documents, whether real, virtual or indexes, look similar to the reader and are contained within the same addressing scheme.

To follow a link, a reader clicks with a mouse (or types in a number if he or she has no mouse). To search [an] index, a reader gives keywords (or other search criteria). These are the only operations necessary to access the entire world of data.

Information provider view

The WWW browsers can access many existing data systems via existing protocols (FTP, NNTP) or via HTTP and a gateway. In this way, the critical mass of data is quickly exceeded, and the increasing use of the system by readers and information suppliers encourage each other.

Making a web is as simple as writing a few SGML files which point to your existing data. Making it public involves running the FTP or HTTP daemon, and making at least one link into your web from another. In fact, any file available by anonymous FTP can be immediately linked into a web. The very small start-up effort is designed to allow small contributions. At the other end of the scale, large information providers may provide an HTTP server with full text or keyword indexing.

The WWW model gets over the frustrating incompatibilities of data format between suppliers and reader by allowing negotiation of format between a smart browser and a smart server. This should provide a basis for extension into multimedia, and allow those who share application standards to make full use of them across the web.

This summary does not describe the many exciting possibilities opened up by the WWW project, such as efficient document caching, the reduction of redundant out-of-date copies, and the use of knowledge daemons. There is more information in the online project documentation, including some background on hypertext and many technical notes.

Berners-Lee, 1991

The Usenet servers

ISPs and companies installed the Usenet server software on a central server that delivered conferences to individual subscribers, who read messages using a news reader application. Users could also post new articles to the Usenet conferences held on their local server. In turn, that server would push copies of new messages to nearby Usenet servers, each of which would then further propagate those messages. Over several hours or even days, messages 'flooded' across Usenet until every server had a copy.

Very few companies considered Usenet to be an essential service, so the Usenet servers were almost never backed up. Worse still, to free up storage space for new messages, most Usenet servers deleted old messages after a few days. It appeared that large chunks of internet history might have been lost forever.

Rescuing Usenet for posterity

Fortunately, a group of zoologists at the University of Toronto hadn't been quite so negligent. Their department had connected to Usenet as early as 1981, when the entire Usenet system probably had only a few hundred users. Henry Spencer, a highly regarded Unix programmer, was then a member of the department and relied on the Usenet community to help solve technical problems. Spencer was loath to delete old Usenet messages, reasoning that they might contain answers to future problems he might encounter in his work, so he began to back up the Zoology department's Usenet feed onto magnetic tape.

The department continued to back up Usenet for the next ten years, with each tape being deposited in an archive. The archiving ended only when the growth of Usenet traffic began to demand more tapes than the department's budget could justify. The backups then found their way to the University of Western Ontario where David Wiseman, a network administrator, began to transfer some 120 MB of data from the decaying tapes onto hard disk. Wiseman eventually recovered more than two million of the very earliest Usenet messages and came to an agreement with Google over hosting them on its servers.

A second partial set of backups existed in the form of the DejaNews Research Service. DejaNews was the first searchable index of Usenet, but in 2000 it ran out of money and its archives were acquired by Google and rebranded as Google Groups. Google now owned a staggering 700 million Usenet postings, which were largely complete except for the very earliest postings – most of which could be found in Spencer and Wiseman's archive. The combined archive is thought to represent 95% of all the messages ever posted to Usenet.

Usenet postings consisted solely of text and did not take up a great amount of storage space. Almost ten years of Usenet traffic produced only 120 MB of text, which would fill less than a quarter of a CD-ROM.

Activity 11 (self-assessment)

Based on the information in Box 2, why did many companies fail to back up Usenet messages?

Today, many companies fail to back up certain types of data – most commonly email. If you work for a business, it is worth finding out if your employer backs up email messages or if they are considered unimportant.

3.4 Conclusion

This session provided you with an introduction to backing up data. You saw the necessity of making backups and learned about the advantages and disadvantages of various backup technologies.

This session should have helped you with the following learning outcomes.

- Explain the importance of developing methods of preserving data.
- Discuss the role of standards in technology.
- Give examples of data recovery from historical sources.
- Decide on an appropriate strategy for backing up computer data.

Deleting data (and getting it back again)

4

Computer files aren't like paper documents. If you decide to throw one away, you can always recover it in perfect condition. Any file sent to the Windows Recycle Bin (Trash on a Mac) can be recovered by opening the Recycle Bin and dragging the file out again. This is a thoughtful feature implemented by the designers, who recognised that users often delete files only to regret that decision.

It is possible to delete files without using the Recycle Bin. Most operating systems have a text-based command-line interface (Command on Windows, Terminal on Mac and Linux computers) that bypasses it entirely. Uninstaller programs that remove applications from a computer also do not use the Recycle Bin. In both these cases, deletion is final unless special tools are used to retrieve the files.

Files in the Recycle Bin have not been changed in any way, except that they are each given a 'flag' marking them for deletion when the Bin is emptied. The flag is removed if files are removed from the Recycle Bin. When the user empties the Bin, the files it contained appear to vanish from the computer. Searching for them will draw a blank – but the files themselves continue to exist and can be recovered using specialised software tools.

To explain further, hard disks are divided into fixed-sized sectors, each of which can hold a certain amount of data. The physical locations of these sectors are listed in a special table of contents that is stored on the disk or chip. When a file is created, pointers to the physical locations of the sectors containing the data are added to the table. Because the table points to the files, it is known as a pointer table.

A simplified diagram of a hard disk is given in Figure 7. The pointer table is shown on the left. As yet there are no files stored on the disk and the table is empty.

Figure 7   **A schematic diagram of a freshly formatted hard disk**

As soon as the user (or the operating system) begins writing files to the disk, pointers are created in the pointer table that direct the operating system to the appropriate sector of the disk (Figure 8).

Figure 8 **The same hard disk after a file has been saved**

Looking at the same disk after a while (Figure 9), the user has been storing data in two folders (colour-coded green and orange). Unused space on the disk is shown in grey. The pointer table now contains pointers to each of the files on the disk, which the operating system can use to locate the individual files. As you can see, files in the orange folder are scattered across the physical surface of the disk, although as far as the user is concerned they appear to be in the same location.

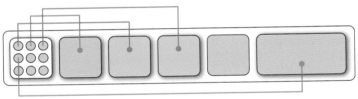

Figure 9 **The hard disk containing files held in two folders**

The user has now chosen to delete one of the green files by placing it in the Recycle Bin (Figure 10). The computer places a flag on that file (a white dot in the figure), showing that it is ready for deletion, but there is no change to the file itself.

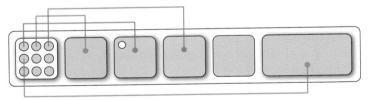

Figure 10 **The hard disk after the user moves one of the files to the Recycle Bin**

When the user actually empties the Recycle Bin (Figure 11), the operating system still does not erase the file itself; instead the pointer in the table is either erased or flagged as no longer needed, meaning that the file cannot be located by the operating system. The file itself continues to exist as a ghost on the disk, but as far as the operating system is concerned, the space formerly occupied by that file is available for storing new data.

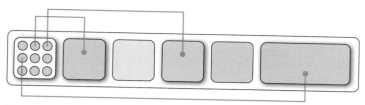

Figure 11 **The hard disk after the Recycle Bin has been emptied**

The file is only completely lost when a new file is written to the same sectors on the disk. A new pointer is created and the data in the original file is lost forever (Figure 12).

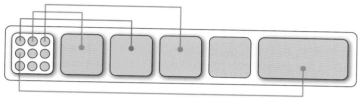

Figure 12 **The hard disk after a new file (coloured pink) has been written to the disk, overwriting the deleted file**

One way of deleting all the data on a disk is to *format* it. After formatting, the disk appears to be completely empty and previous contents have been lost. The most common method of formatting is a high-level format, sometimes called a *quick format*, which can be completed in a few minutes even on very large devices. A high-level format is fast because only the pointers in the location table are erased, making the previous contents invisible to the computer's operating system (see Figure 13). The data itself remains intact on the disk, but it is inaccessible to the operating system.

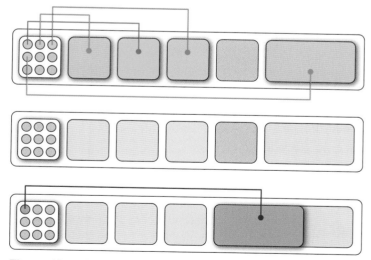

Figure 13 **The same disk before (top) and after (middle) a quick format; new files (bottom) can be written to the drive, overwriting the old data, but large chunks of data remain present and can potentially be recovered**

4.1   Retrieving deleted data

The ghostly traces of deleted data on disks are called *data remanence* and they can be valuable – both to law enforcement officials and to criminals. The data can be recovered using specialised software tools. Disks formatted using Microsoft's DOS format (Windows machines and most memory cards) support *undelete* programs or utilities that can be used in cases where files have been deleted, but the disk has not been formatted. When a file is deleted in DOS, its pointers are marked as being no longer needed. The undelete program finds these flagged pointers and follows them to the physical location of the deleted data, which is then copied to a new file.

The undeleting process has limitations:

- If the operating system has written a file to the same location on the disk, some or all of the previously deleted data will have been overwritten. The likelihood that deleted data has been lost is dependent on a number of factors. Generally, the longer the time elapsed between deleting the file and attempting recovery, the greater the likelihood that part of the disk has been reused.

- The fuller the disk, the greater the chances that the deleted file has been overwritten. My simplified diagrams suggest that files are stored as single blocks on disks; in reality a single file can be fragmented across many blocks, which slows down the reading and writing of files. Such *fragmentation* makes it more likely that a deleted file will be overwritten by a piece of a new file. The unimaginatively named 'defragmenting process' (often shortened to 'defragging') reduces fragmentation by joining parts of files together so they occupy uninterrupted areas of the disk (Box 3). During defragmentation large amounts of data are relocated, making it extremely likely that previously deleted data is overwritten.

Activity 12 (self-assessment)

A user of a Windows computer accidentally deletes a file and wants to recover it. How could they get their data back:

(a) before emptying the Recycle Bin

(b) after emptying the Bin?

Activity 13 (self-assessment)

Give one piece of advice to a colleague who has accidentally deleted a file from their Windows computer and then emptied the Recycle Bin.

Box 3 Defragmenting

Mac OS X and other Unix-based operating systems continuously perform small amounts of defragmenting whenever the computer is switched on. Inevitably, previously deleted data is constantly being overwritten while the machine is used. There is no simple 'undelete' on Unix machines; instead, specialist software must be used to try and recover data.

Windows Vista and 7 defragment their disks at set intervals (usually in the middle of the night when it is less likely that the computer will be busy). You can find the defragmenter tool by typing *defrag* into the Start menu search bar.

Older versions of Windows do not automatically defragment their disks. On these operating systems the Windows defragger can be found by right-clicking on a hard disk's icon, choosing Properties, then Tools and choosing Defragment Now.

Defragging is a time-consuming and processor-intensive process, best done when you are not going to be using your computer. There is a small risk that defragmentation might fail, or crash during the reorganisation of your disk, so you should always back up your data beforehand.

Activity 14 (self-assessment)

A friend has accidentally deleted some files from their computer. They have bought an undelete utility. Should they install the application to their computer?

4.2 Deleting data forever

As you have seen, a quick format leaves intact data on the drive. Even for computers not using the DOS format, data can be recovered using specialised software such as that used by professional data recovery companies. This means that when computers are disposed of, their hard disks may contain financially or personally valuable information – with a risk that their next owner could recover that information and misuse it.

Before a computer is sent for disposal, its owners can protect themselves by ensuring that no data is sent away with the computer. One method is simply to retain the hard disks for future use and dispose of the remainder of the computer – but obviously that affects the resale value and attractiveness of the machine. Some other methods include:

- *Overwriting (wiping or shredding) the disk.* Some disk management programs provide an 'overwrite' utility that fills every part of the disk

The intensity of magnetic fields (such as those representing data in magnetic media) is measured in units called gauss (abbreviated G). The unit is named after the German mathematician, astronomer and physicist Carl Friedrich Gauss (1777–1855), who explored many aspects of magnetism.

with zeros, ones or a random mix of the two. In theory this extremely time-consuming process completely obliterates any trace of the previous data. Fortunately, hard disks can safely be overwritten with a single pass of an *overwriting* utility. However, research has shown that it is possible to recover data from floppy disks that have been overwritten a single time; in such cases multiple overwrites are needed to guarantee that the data has been destroyed. Some operating systems support 'secure file delete', which deletes a file and then performs an overwrite of the section of the disk formerly occupied by the file.

- *Degaussing the disk.* Data on hard and floppy disks or magnetic tape is stored in patterns of magnetisation. These patterns can be disrupted by a powerful magnetic field, and a sufficiently powerful field can erase an entire disk in a few minutes – a process known as *degaussing*. A disk or tape that has been properly degaussed can safely be reused or disposed of.

  Degaussing requires extremely expensive equipment and expert supervision to be effective. The increased reliability of modern magnetic storage media has been achieved by making them resistant to stray magnetic fields – which requires that even stronger magnetic fields must be used in the degausser. Improper degaussing leaves enough magnetisation on the medium that some or all of the data can be recovered.

- *Physical destruction.* Some organisations cannot tolerate the risk that overwriting software might not be completely effective or that disks will not be properly degaussed. Instead, they require that the storage media are completely destroyed when no longer needed. Incineration is the most popular method of destroying storage media (though it must be performed in a specially designed facility – most storage devices either contain toxic substances or produce them when burned), but they can also be crushed or shredded. Some household paper shredders are capable of destroying CDs and DVDs.

4.3 Deleting remote data

So far you have seen that it is possible to delete data permanently from a hard disk or other physical device. *In extremis* you could guarantee that the data was irretrievably lost by taking a hammer to the disk! Yet all these techniques only work if you actually possess the device holding the data. How can you guarantee that data held elsewhere on the internet is actually deleted?

Before you spend too long wondering about the solution, the answer is – you can't. Whenever you use services provided by another organisation, you lose control of your data. Reputable providers all give legally binding assurances that they do not retain information any longer than you require, but there is no simple way of confirming if this is the case.

Activity 15 (exploratory)

Google Docs is an example of a cloud application that you have already used during your studies. In the resources page associated with this part on the TU100 website you will find a link to Google's privacy policy, which explains how data is deleted from the system. Does Google remove data from its servers as soon as the user deletes a file?

Organisations requiring absolute control of their data will build and operate their own offsite backups rather than entrust the data to others, or ensure that all data held offsite is hidden by powerful encryption technologies (you will learn more about encryption in a later part). Yet we do not just *deliberately* create data on remote computers – a great deal of our activity on the internet results in the creation of data, often without us knowing. This data can contain personal information, or it can be linked back to an individual.

If someone asked me to explain computer networks in one sentence, I'd first of all struggle and then come up with something along the lines of:

> a set of connections between computers that allow data to be moved from machine to machine.

This is pretty accurate – if I write an email on my computer and press the Send button, it will eventually appear in a colleague's inbox. The email *appears* to have moved from my machine to theirs. However, an equally accurate explanation of networks is:

> a set of connections between computers that allow data to be *copied* from machine to machine.

Going back to my email example:

1 Whilst I edit the email, copies of the text are saved to a folder on my hard disk called Drafts; clicking on the Send button transmits a *copy* of the message to The Open University's outgoing mail server.

2 As soon as the mail server acknowledges that it has received the message, my computer moves the draft text to the Sent folder.

3 The OU's outgoing mail server now tries to deliver the message to the recipient's incoming mail server. The message is kept on the server's disk until it is successfully delivered. Although the OU does not do so, it would not be difficult for the operators of an outgoing mail server to keep copies of all the messages passing through that machine.

4 A copy of the message is now stored on the recipient's mail server, where it remains until the user decides to retrieve their mail.

5 When the recipient downloads their messages, they too have a local copy of the email. The copy on their mail server may also be retained.

If the email is sent to a server outside the OU, it might be routed from computer to computer until it reaches its destination. At each point, copies of the message are made and can be retained for some time. An increasing number of governments, employers and ISPs are choosing to retain some or all of the information we send over computer networks. A pessimistic view of the future is that we will have less and less control over our data, becoming ever more reliant on the law and good faith to protect our data from misuse. You will return to these issues of privacy and the law in a later part.

4.4 Conclusion

In this session you learned how computers delete data and that deletion need not be permanent. You were introduced to the workings of the DOS operating system and how it makes it possible to recover files using an undelete utility.

You were also given some guidelines for the safe destruction of data and computer hardware so as to minimise the risk of valuable information being misused by other people.

This session should have helped you with the following learning outcomes.

- Describe how operating systems manage data.
- Discuss the value of the long-term persistence of data.

Investigating data

5

An increasing number of legal actions rely on evidence in the form of computer data. The investigation of computer data in order to obtain legal evidence is known as *forensic computing*, *computer forensics* or *digital forensics*.

5.1 Securing a computer

Forensics experts use the analogy of a medic arriving at the scene of an accident – the 'first response'. Whenever it is suspected that a computer might contain valuable information that could be used in a civil or criminal case, a number of steps should be taken to secure the data (obviously these should be taken only with the proper authority). This process is known as *imaging* a disk.

1   The computer is immediately powered off. Perhaps surprisingly, the computer is not switched off by logging out of the operating system and then shutting down power. Instead it is quite normal to flick the power switch or remove the battery, causing the computer to shut down immediately. This is because when a user logs out of a computer or shuts it down using a menu option, there is a short pause before they are disconnected or the machine is powered off. During this time the computer writes a very large amount of information to the hard disk; it might also be locking and unlocking files and deleting information such as the list of visited websites or temporary files used by applications. An immediate power-off keeps all of these files intact, allowing them to be examined at a later date. Obviously, any data held only in RAM will be lost when power is disconnected.

2   The hard disk is removed from the computer and sent to a secure facility for examination. Such facilities may be operated by law-enforcement organisations (such as the police) or more often by small, specialist companies.

3   An exact copy (or *image*) is made of all the information on the original disk. The disk is set to allow only read access; this can be done either by a special piece of hardware that attaches to the drive's cable, or by software on disk. Special copying software is then used to duplicate the exact structure of the suspect disk, including deleted files that are no longer accessible to the operating system and any information that might have been stored in areas of the disk outside that used by the operating system.

You will learn more about hashes in a later part.

4   A program calculates a unique mathematical 'fingerprint' (known as the *hash*) of the original drive's contents. A hash is a sequence of numbers and letters that can only correspond to the exact contents and layout of the drive, and so it is used to authenticate computer data.

5   The original drive is placed in a safe.

6   Further copies of the duplicate drive are sent to all interested parties – such as the prosecution and defence teams – along with the value of the hash. Each of the parties then calculates the value of the hash on their drive. If the drive is an accurate copy of the original disk then their hash value will be identical to that on the suspect drive. If the hashes vary then the party owning the copy knows that either files have been modified on their drive or the copying process was faulty, in which case they can request another copy to be made from the original disk.

7   The copies of the drives are then examined using further forensic tools.

Activity 16 (self-assessment)

What purpose do the mathematical hashes serve in a forensic examination?

5.2   Metadata

Computers not only contain data representing text files, images, films, sounds and so on; they also contain data about that data. This additional, hidden data is known as *metadata*. You can see some of this metadata by viewing the information about a file. On a Windows machine, right-click on a file and choose Properties from the pop-up menu; on an Apple Macintosh, right-click on the file and choose Get Info. The new window that opens will show you a large amount of information about the file you have selected.

Activity 17 (exploratory)

Choose a file on your computer and examine its metadata using the method described above. List the information you see, then briefly explain which pieces of information you think might be useful in a forensic investigation.

Comment

Using Windows 7 I was able to obtain the following information:

1   the name of the file

2   the type of file and what application could open it

3   its location on the disk

4   the size of the file

5   when the file was created, when it was last modified and when it was last accessed

6   the ownership of the file and which users could read or modify it.

The last two pieces of information would be extremely useful in a forensic examination as they could be used to determine who had access to a file and when it was used. Far more information about files is available using more advanced features inside Windows and/or specialist software.

5.3   Some simple forensic techniques

Whenever a computer is running, both the operating system and the applications keep records of actions in text documents known as *log files*. Even a humble PC can have many hundreds of log files recording actions, a few of which could include:

- when the computer has been switched on and powered off
- the names of users who have logged in to the computer, when they logged in and when they logged out
- the times, dates and durations of any network connections
- records of which software has been installed, deleted and updated and when any changes were made
- the names of applications that have crashed and when it happened
- the times and dates when the computer tried to access a peripheral device such as a printer.

During normal use, we do not need to worry about log files; the operating system will regularly replace old entries with new ones. The only time most of us ever refer to a log file is when a computer or an application is faulty; in which case the log will contain detailed information describing the errors that caused the failure. Figure 14 shows a log file that was generated when a program crashed during installation. Much of the data is extremely technical and really only of use to developers, but the log does include simple information such as the name and version of the software that crashed, the name and version of the operating system being used and the time and date of the crash.

Activity 18 (exploratory)

In the resources page associated with this part on the TU100 website, you will find a video that shows the beginning of a forensic investigation of a hard disk image. When convenient, go to the website and watch this video.

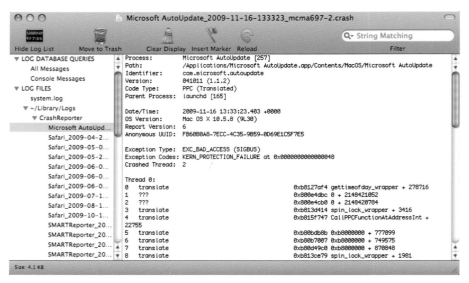

Figure 14 **An example of a log file on the Mac OS X operating system**

5.4 Disaster data

France's accident investigation agency has abandoned a search for the 'black boxes' from the Air France passenger jet that crashed in the Atlantic Ocean.

The research ship leading the hunt had left the area of the crash and would soon arrive in Senegal, concluding the "second phase" of the effort, it said.

Experts will gather in the coming weeks to decide whether to launch a third.

The Airbus A330 crashed in a storm en route from Rio de Janeiro to Paris on 1 June, killing all 228 people on board.

(BBC News, 2009)

You will probably have heard of 'black boxes' fitted to airliners and how they can be used to recover vital information about the cause of a disaster. *Flight data recorders (FDRs)*, as they are properly known, were invented in 1939; but their use was only seriously considered after the world's first jet airliner, the Comet 1, was involved in a series of in-flight disasters. Today FDRs are required by law in all passenger aircraft. They constantly record more than eighty parameters – including airspeed, heading, flight control positions and engine information – to a magnetic tape or (more recently) solid memory.

The FDR is designed to survive almost any conceivable disaster and its safe recovery is one of the first objectives after the immediate rescue of people from a crash. It is then transferred to a secure facility where its

Later testing revealed that the Comet's fuselage was extremely prone to metal fatigue, which would eventually cause the aircraft to disintegrate at high altitude.

contents can be duplicated and played back, allowing crash investigators to 'relive' the last few minutes of the flight. Box 4 describes how such a 'black box' was used to learn more about the causes of the *Columbia* disaster.

Box 4 The *Columbia* disaster

The space shuttle orbiter *Columbia* disintegrated during re-entry to the Earth's atmosphere on 1 February 2003. Remarkably, data was recovered from the wreckage that helped to solve the mystery of her loss.

Shortly after take-off, *Columbia* was hit by a chunk of insulation that was shed from her fuel tank. The light foam smashed a hole in the ship's protective heat tiles, allowing hot gas to enter and destroy *Columbia*'s wing.

Within hours of the disaster, NASA were confident that the loss of *Columbia* had been caused by a failure of the spacecraft's insulating tiles, but they could not identify where the initial breach had been located. *Columbia* was not only the oldest shuttle, but had been the test vehicle for the fleet. Uniquely, she was wired with over seven hundred sensors that recorded every aspect of her behaviour. This modular auxiliary data system, known as MADS, constantly recorded data onto magnetic tape that would be examined when the shuttle returned to Earth.

There was a possibility that some of MADS might have survived the devastating loss of the ship, the sudden deceleration and the final plummet to Earth. The first problem was finding MADS: it was somewhere inside a debris field more than 80 km wide and 1000 km long that stretched across three states. Six weeks after the disaster, MADS was located near Hemphill, Texas. Incredibly, MADS was almost intact.

The recorder was flown to Minnesota and carefully disassembled by data storage experts. The tape was removed and cleaned to remove any contamination from the environment. It was then flown to the Kennedy Space Center in Florida, where it was duplicated and the original carefully stored. One of the copies was sent to the Johnson Space Center in Houston for further analysis.

Using the MADS data it was possible to make a second-by-second reconstruction of events on the orbiter. Pressure sensors inside the wing had recorded a sudden blow at the time of the original impact, followed a little later by temperature sensors noticing unusual changes in temperature deep inside the spacecraft that should not have occurred. During re-entry MADS faithfully recorded a series of failures in *Columbia*'s systems as hot gas gradually burned through cables and pipes and began to heat up the structure of the ship. The sequence of failures allowed NASA to come to a firm conclusion as to the cause of the disaster that was in agreement with what had been seen from the ground, the data sent from the shuttle itself and the debris.

> If it had been a shuttle other than Columbia, we would still be having this debate. The Columbia had that [MADS] instrumentation, and the Lord provided that box for us, and within three or four days of analyzing that data, everybody started to converge on what had to be [a breach in] the leading edge. So, we got over this denial stuff.
>
> Frank Buzzard, Director of NASA task force supporting the Columbia Accident Investigation Board, quoted in Cabbage and Harwood, 2004, p. 228

The investigation was concluded after NASA performed an experiment in which a chunk of insulating foam about the size of that which hit the shuttle was fired at wing sections identical to those on *Columbia*. To the horror of everyone who saw it, the foam easily penetrated the shuttle's heat shield.

A video recording taken by one of the astronauts during re-entry was salvaged from the wreckage. The last few minutes of the tape were completely destroyed by heat, but the earlier part of the video was recoverable. None of the surviving footage or data suggests that any of the astronauts were aware of any problems with *Columbia* until the spacecraft began to disintegrate.

5.5 Conclusion

In this session you learned that techniques exist that can recover data in almost any circumstances. You learned a little about how forensic computing investigations are conducted and saw the importance of metadata in reconstructing how a computer system has been used.

Many of these techniques have been developed for forensics purposes involving crime or disaster, but it is worth remembering that these same techniques could be used to intrude on a person's privacy or for criminal purposes.

This session should have helped you with the following learning outcome.

- Describe how computer data can be protected in the event of a criminal or civil investigation.

Designing data to last

6

You have already seen how data can be physically preserved almost indefinitely by a combination of durable media, regular duplication and distribution; but this does not solve the problem of data losing its meaning through technological obsolescence.

We can ensure that data remains *meaningful* by describing how it has been designed and publishing that description as widely as possible. Such descriptions are known as *standards*. The modern world is full of standards; you have already met several during this module, including TCP, IP, HTML, XML and the family of wireless standards grouped together as 802.11. Beyond TU100, almost every aspect of your life is governed by standards – they are responsible for guaranteeing that machines work as expected, that food, drink and energy supplies (Box 5) meet acceptable guidelines, and that devices can be expected to work with one another. In fact, we rely on standards so much that we rarely think of the consequences when there are none in place.

6.1 Proprietary computing formats

The main text for this module was written using The Open University's preferred word processor, Microsoft Word. The OU adopted Word nearly 20 years ago, not only because it offered the greatest range of functionality but also because Word was beginning to dominate the business market. Word and the other Microsoft Office applications have been extremely profitable for Microsoft's Business Division; in 2008 alone it sold more than US$18 billion worth of software.

For most of its history, Word stored documents in the DOC format that was developed by Microsoft. Word DOC files not only contain text and pictures, they include a great deal of information used to style and lay out a document. This information allows Word users to create and exchange complex documents with other Word users on a range of computing platforms. There should be no problems for users so long as they are content to exchange files with fellow Word users. Difficulties begin when a file must be exchanged with someone who does not use Word.

Until early 2008, Microsoft refused to publish the exact specification of a DOC file. Without this information, it was almost impossible to write programs that could read or write DOC files. External developers wishing to include DOC support in their programs could pay a licence fee to

Box 5 Electrical supplies

When travelling abroad, one of the items you will almost certainly put in your luggage is a travel adaptor allowing you to plug your electrical items into local wall sockets. If you have travelled widely then you will probably have noticed the wide variety of sockets (Figure 15) and voltages (Figure 16) that can be found in different countries, all apparently doing the same job. Today there are thirteen, usually incompatible, socket designs in use; moreover in a few countries, such as Brazil, India and China, more than one type of electrical network is in use.

Electrical supplies in many countries were developed by local industries, which excluded foreign competition by designing their own electrical systems. In most countries there is a single electrical system using the same voltage, frequency and plugs, but this has not always been the case. Historically, individual power companies protected their markets by developing incompatible electrical networks.

It is only some 80 years since the UK adopted a single standard for mains electricity; before then, power companies delivered electricity as either AC or DC current, at different voltages and frequencies, and requiring different plugs. By 1918 in London alone, there were some 70 power companies using 50 different electrical systems, 10 different frequencies and 24 different voltages!

Activity 19 (exploratory)

In the resources page associated with this part on the TU100 website, you will find a short video clip from the BBC television series *James May's 20th Century* explaining how the UK came to standardise its electrical system. Watch this clip, and try to note down the main benefit to (a) customers and (b) manufacturers of the UK adopting a single voltage and socket system for mains electricity.

Comment

(a) Consumers could buy an appliance confident that it could be used in any electrical socket in the country.

(b) Manufacturers could build electrical appliances that used a single voltage and plug rather than having to make a number of devices for different systems. Their costs were reduced and the potential market for their goods increased.

Standardisation meant that electrical appliances became cheaper and more attractive to consumers, so demand increased.

Since 1988, mains electricity has been standardised across the European Union in terms of both voltage (230 V) and frequency (50 Hz). However, the design of plugs has *not* been standardised (Europe uses types C, E, F and G), requiring people to carry adaptors when travelling between some countries.

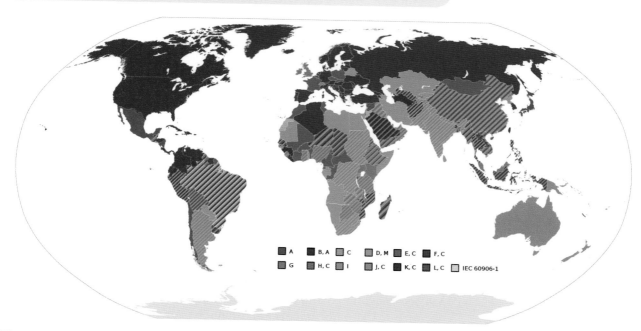

Figure 15 Map of the different types of electrical plug and socket used around the world: each type of plug and socket is known by a different letter from A to M (for instance, the UK uses type G)

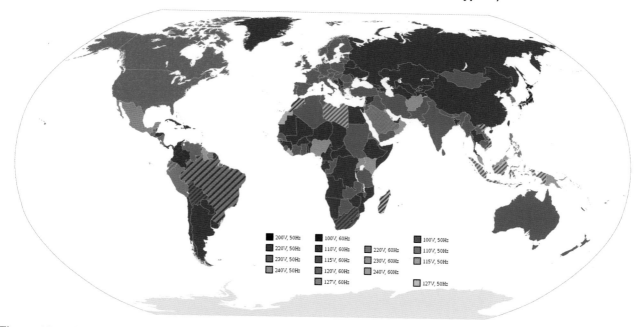

Figure 16 Map of the different electrical voltages and frequencies used around the world

Microsoft, for which they would be given the specification. Alternatively, they could attempt to work out the DOC specification without Microsoft's help, but the results were somewhat hit and miss. Microsoft eventually made the full specification for DOC available in 2008, allowing other software companies to write products supporting Word documents.

Even though anyone can now write programs that can read and write DOC files, the file format is still Microsoft's property. No other company is permitted to make changes to DOC, even if those changes would greatly improve its usefulness.

Because Microsoft created and still controls the DOC format, we call DOC a *proprietary format*.

6.2 Formal standards

Proprietary formats give their owners enormous power. They can exclude competitors from a market and force users to buy a particular piece of software or hardware. However, just as the standardisation of electrical supplies mentioned in Box 5 helped to increase the market for electronics, standardisation of hardware and software can increase the market for such products.

When a number of companies or trade bodies agree on a standard, it is known as a *formal standard*. This means that every aspect of the standard has been negotiated and recorded in what is known as a standards document. These documents are exhaustive (and exhausting) descriptions of every aspect of a standard, often running to many hundreds of pages of detail. As an example, the specification for the Adobe PDF standard used by many document readers grew from a novel-length document of 390 pages in 1996 to a blockbusting 1236 pages ten years later.

You might be wondering why the PDF specification has changed and continued to grow. The answer is that PDF started off as a relatively simple format allowing print-quality documents to be exchanged between computers irrespective of their operating system or software. Since its introduction it has accumulated a large number of additional features, including improved colour and font handling, security for exchanging confidential information and multimedia support. Each of these additions needed to be fully set out in the formal PDF specification.

Until July 2008, the PDF document format was a proprietary format wholly owned by Adobe. Software developers wishing to write software that could read or write PDF documents had to purchase a licence from Adobe, in exchange for which they would be able to legally incorporate PDF support into their products. Any company that did not pay for a licence could be prosecuted for infringing Adobe's intellectual property.

In July 2008 the PDF 1.7 standard was accepted as an international standard known as ISO/IEC 32000-1:2008. PDF is now an *open format* or open standard – one that anyone is free to use or develop for without paying a licence fee to Adobe. Future revisions to the PDF standard can be proposed by any party.

It might seem surprising that a company would give away the result of many years' hard work, but in fact PDF licences represented only a tiny part of Adobe's income. The company makes a huge amount of money from selling expensive professional software products such as Photoshop, Illustrator and Acrobat – and all these programs can generate PDF documents. Adobe takes the strategic view that the more products there are using PDF, the greater the demand for Adobe's development tools.

Adobe may also be trying to safeguard against threats to PDF as a document format. Rival companies might have been willing to invest money into competing formats when there was an opportunity to earn lucrative licensing fees from developers; however, now that PDF is free, developers are unlikely to choose to licence a proprietary format instead of an open standard.

Activity 20 (self-assessment)

What are the two main advantages for Adobe in making PDF an open standard rather than a proprietary one?

Standards are regulated by a large number of organisations operating on an industry-wide, national or international basis, as shown in Table 2.

Table 2   Examples of organisations that regulate standards

Scope	Example	Role
Industry-wide	European Computer Manufacturers Association – Ecma International	Regulating standards for information and communications systems
National	British Standards Institution (BSI)	Production of standards for the British market
International	International Organisation for Standardisation (ISO)	Production and promotion of international standards

Many standards begin life as a specification designed by one company or organisation that gradually assumes a dominant role within an industry. Such specifications may then be referred to a national or international standards body for certification. As a result, a single standard might be known by several names. The World Wide Web Consortium's standard

HTML 4.01 has also been approved as an international standard and is sometimes called ISO HTML, or more precisely ISO/IEC 15445:2000.

Word becomes a standard

Microsoft Word's DOC format had been designed when people were happy only to print or read word-processed documents from their screens, but by 2000 Microsoft customers were demanding that Word documents could be fed directly into databases or stock-control programs rather than the data having to be laboriously copied by hand.

DOC was inadequate for this task, so Microsoft began to examine the possibility of replacing DOC with XML. To recap briefly, XML allows developers to create specific tags that identify elements within a document as having a specific meaning. A document saved in XML is made up from nothing more than tagged text; it can even be opened in a text editor. The set of valid tags is defined in a suitable schema (which can be thought of as being equivalent to the stylesheets used by Word to format text). Users would see no difference between a new XML-aware word-processor and previous versions, but the program would operate in a completely different manner; it would use the document's schema to draw the tagged content of the XML document using the appropriate fonts and pagination.

XML could go even further. Programs capable of reading XML did not need to slavishly reproduce the appearance of the text; they could extract information from the document using the document's tags. A simple program could parse, or analyse, a document that contained tags identifying names, addresses, phone numbers and email addresses and copy that information to an address book; likewise, it would be trivial to extract images, tables, hyperlinks and citations from one document and put them into another.

Microsoft first began work on an XML format for its Office suite in 2000, and introduced it to customers in 2003 as Microsoft Office XML. A very simple Office XML document is shown below. When opened in Microsoft Office 2003 or later (or another program capable of reading Office 2003 XML), it displays the message Hello World!

```
<?xml version="1.0"?>
<?mso-application progid="Word.Document"?>
<w:wordDocument xmlns:w="http://schemas.microsoft.com/office/
word/2003/wordml">
    <w:body>
        <w:p>
        <w:r>
        <w:t>Hello, World!</w:t>
        </w:r>
        </w:p>
    </w:body>
</w:wordDocument>
```

You should immediately recognise the structure of the document from your experience with HTML. There are clear pairs of tags identifying parts of the document, although their names will not be familiar to you – `<w:p>` is an Office XML tag for 'paragraph', whilst `<w:t>` is the tag for 'text' and so on. Obviously, a large Office XML document will contain many tens of thousands of lines of tagged content and will be associated with a large schema describing how it is to be processed.

The full benefits of Office XML would become apparent only if software companies other than Microsoft committed to supporting it in their products. Microsoft could simply licence Office XML, but traditionally many companies are reluctant to pay licence fees for products that might change at any time and give them no control over any future changes. It made sense for Microsoft to make Office XML as widely available as possible.

In 2004, the European Union recommended that document-publishing software sold within the EU should offer greater interoperability, allowing users to switch between applications without risking loss of data. The benefit of XML was that users would not be restricted to using documents inside their word processor; *any* XML-aware application could read the document. The user could even switch to an alternative word processor and not only be able to open the file, but also be sure it would be a faithful version of that seen in the original program. Responding to the EU, Microsoft proposed that Office XML should become an agreed open standard under the control of a private international standards body – Ecma International.

Ecma began the process of standardisation by forming a working group to examine the Office XML specification (which was more than 2000 pages long). The group was made up from industry specialists, representatives of the British Library and the United States Library of Congress, and the GNOME Foundation – a non-profit organisation dedicated to developing free software. The Office XML specification eventually grew to more than 6000 pages before it was ratified as the open standard ECMA-376 in December 2006. The Office XML standard was then scrutinised by ISO under its 'fast track' approval process. After two years of amendments it became international standard ISO/IEC 29500:2008. A very lengthy process!

Ecma was originally founded as the European Computer Manufacturers Association. Its members are drawn from computer and telecommunications industries operating inside Europe as well as research facilities and non-profit organisations.

Activity 21 (self-assessment)

What was the benefit to software developers of Office XML becoming an open standard?

6.3 De facto standards

The development of Office Open XML is an example of the official standardisation process, but standards can also develop in an informal manner as one technology becomes dominant over rivals. These are known as *de facto standards* and are surprisingly commonplace; some examples in everyday life are:

- the arrangement of the clutch, brake and accelerator pedals in cars, which is independent of the manufacturer
- the fact that screw lids are tightened by turning them clockwise
- the QWERTY keyboard on your computer.

Another example of a de facto standard is the IBM PC-compatible computers that dominate the market for personal computers (although the term 'PC-compatible' is rapidly being replaced by 'Windows computer'). PC compatibles are an enormous family of machines made over 30 years by thousands of manufacturers that can, for the most part, run the same applications. However, at no time has there ever been such a thing as an agreed formal PC specification. Instead, the dominance of the PC came about almost by accident.

In the early days the personal computer market was largely created by, and dominated by, Apple. IBM was slow to realise the enormous potential of the microcomputer, but in 1980 it set to work on Project Chess, the IBM 5150 personal computer.

IBM took little more than a year to bring the PC to market. The company was able to achieve this only by turning its back on its traditional methods. In the past IBM had built almost every component in its machines, but the IBM PC was assembled from existing, readily available parts and software sourced from outside the company (Box 6 describes the impact this had on one familiar organisation). IBM's only significant new contribution to the PC was its proprietary Basic Input/Output System (BIOS), the software used to start the computer and prepare it for use.

Box 6 Microsoft and the IBM PC

The biggest beneficiary of IBM's approach to designing the PC was a small Seattle-based software company called Microsoft. Every PC sold by IBM ran Microsoft's MS-DOS operating system, and every sale resulted in a small royalty fee going to Microsoft. Crucially, Microsoft's contract with IBM was non-exclusive; Microsoft was perfectly entitled to offer MS-DOS to other manufacturers – and it did. By 1994 Microsoft had sold over 100 million copies of MS-DOS and established itself as one of the largest software companies in the world.

If the PC were to be a success it would have to outsell the then market leader, the Apple II. IBM's strategy was that the PC would flourish if it was supplied with a large number of peripheral and software manufacturers. In contrast to Apple's strict licensing regulations, the IBM PC used an open architecture; companies could develop hardware and software for the PC without paying licence fees to IBM. To speed development, IBM sold the *IBM PC Technical Reference Manual*, an engineering and programming guide to the computer including complete circuit diagrams and a listing of the source code for the BIOS.

Activity 22 (self-assessment)

Some aspects of the original IBM PC can be described as 'open', others as 'proprietary'. Give some examples of each.

When it went on sale in 1981, the IBM PC proved to be a huge success. IBM began to earn a fortune and rival companies wanted a share of that market. Since the PC was built from off-the-shelf components, it would have been a relatively simple task for competitors to assemble a machine physically identical to those rolling off the IBM production lines. Yet that would not have made it a PC. The IBM machines were only PCs because of the proprietary BIOS software. In order to run all PC software, any 'PC-compatible' machine would have to use BIOS software; but the BIOS was IBM's property and they weren't selling it to anyone.

Despite that, in late 1982 Columbia Data Products (CDP) released the MPC 1600, a computer that could run any application written for the IBM PC. CDP had neither licensed IBM's BIOS nor broken the law; instead, it had written a completely new (although functionally indistinguishable) BIOS of its own (see Box 7). CDP's engineers had taken the PC's BIOS source code from the reference manual and used it to write a completely new BIOS specification. CDP's specification was then carefully examined by lawyers to ensure it contained nothing that could be traced back to IBM's engineers. The new specification was then passed on to a programming team who had no experience of IBM's own PC BIOS. Their resulting BIOS behaved identically to IBM's, although it was programmed in a completely different manner.

A host of other manufacturers, most notably Compaq (now part of Hewlett-Packard), soon followed CDP's route and produced their own BIOS programs. PC-compatibles had been born.

> ### Box 7 How to copy a design – legally
>
> The process of producing functionally identical copies of existing hardware and software is known as *clean room design* (sometimes called Chinese wall design). The technique has been used to copy both software and hardware. Clean room design allows companies to catch up with rivals, but leaves them vulnerable to allegations of simply stealing the originator's work.

Activity 23 (self-assessment)

Which three decisions made by the team behind the IBM PC made it possible for other companies to copy their design?

Within a couple of years of its introduction, the IBM PC accounted for only a tiny share of the booming IBM PC-compatible industry, which by then took up more than 90% of the computer market. Ironically, IBM probably made more money from the PC becoming a standard outside its control than it would have made from making expensive IBM PCs intended for the business market. After initially attempting to dissuade manufacturers from copying its machine, IBM actively courted PC makers, encouraging them to license other IBM technologies. Competition quickly reduced the cost of PCs, making them affordable to many more people than IBM could have dreamed of. IBM continued to make PCs until 2004, when the IBM PC division was sold to the Chinese manufacturer Lenovo for US$1.75 billion.

The problem with de facto standards

The IBM PC standard is completely informal; there are no controlling bodies and companies can choose to diverge from it as they see fit. When these changes are made, the result can be unreliable or disappointing for the user.

Both Intel and Microsoft have made regular attempts to regulate the PC industry. Both companies regularly issue 'reference' documents that lay down guidelines on how a PC should be designed, and provide advance information about upcoming hardware and software.

However, such is the diversity of hardware suppliers and software companies in the PC market that it is the much larger Microsoft, in particular, that is forced to try and accommodate their wishes. Microsoft Windows supports many tens of thousands of pieces of hardware and software through specialised programs known as drivers, most of which are written by companies other than Microsoft. The complexity of handling so many drivers, some of which are poorly programmed, is responsible for many of Windows' supposed failings. In actuality, the core parts of Windows are generally extremely well programmed and have relatively few bugs.

A contrasting approach is that of Apple, which builds the hardware from a limited range of standard components and writes the operating system to support those devices only. Apple has attracted a (not always deserved) reputation for reliability, but this is at the expense of consumer choice.

6.4 Conclusion

Standards are one way of ensuring that data can be spread and utilised as widely as possible. They allow information to be used on a variety of systems and help to offset the possibility of technological and digital obsolescence.

In this session two types of standard were discussed. The first, formal standards, are constructed over long periods of time by large numbers of people. Formal standards are agreed and regulated by industry-wide, national and international organisations. The process is time-consuming and very expensive. Formal standards appear very slowly and may persist for many years.

The second type, de facto standards, occur when one particular technology becomes dominant in a market. Some de facto standards arise from one supplier, whilst others are created when more than one company settles on a common design. De facto standards are unregulated, and products do not always meet the standard. De facto standards also change more quickly than formal standards, or even cease to apply over very short periods of time.

This session should have helped you with the following learning outcomes.

- Describe how standards are developed.
- Discuss the role of standards in technology.

7

Preserving data – forever

Earlier in this part of the block you saw how no existing storage technology can guarantee that data will last indefinitely. Instead it is necessary to make faithful copies of data before time and the environment can render it useless. So long as we are prepared to accept the cost and effort involved in making these copies, data can last indefinitely. If it is stored in a standard format, there is no reason why it cannot remain intact for all time. This session will look at two projects that aim to preserve data forever.

7.1   The Wayback Machine

Websites change at an incredible rate as companies adopt new technologies (such as Adobe Flash), rebrand themselves, are taken over by competitors, fail, or simply redesign their pages. It is relatively simple to change the code or graphics for a website and transform it beyond recognition; in the process, the previous version is often consigned to the Recycle Bin. With the Web it's even possible to rewrite history; a page containing erroneous, out-of-date or simply inconvenient data can be removed without leaving a trace.

The Wayback Machine is a project from a non-profit organisation, the Internet Foundation, based in San Francisco and hosted by the Library of Congress. It takes 'snapshots' of websites and adds them to its archive, allowing users to view sites as they appeared at various times in the past. The interval between snapshots means that the Wayback Machine cannot possibly collect every change to the Web, but it does give a broad overview of how it has developed.

As you can imagine, an extraordinary amount of data is being gathered by the Wayback Machine. In 2003 it was collecting approximately 12 TB every month; by 2009 the rate of increase was 100 TB every month and the whole project had collected 3 petabytes (PB) of data.

1 petabyte (PB) is 2^{10} (1024) terabytes or 2^{20} gigabytes.

Activity 24 (exploratory)

The Wayback Machine is a fascinating glimpse of the Web as it used to be. In the resources page associated with this part on the TU100 website, you will find instructions on how to explore it.

7.2 The Long Now

The Long Now Foundation, based in San Francisco, is a non-profit group that is trying to raise awareness of the chronically short-term nature of most human planning, and to encourage developers to design their products in such a way that they will be useful into the indefinite future.

One of the Long Now's projects concerns the loss of knowledge through the dramatic rate of extinction in human languages. The Rosetta Project is a global collaboration between linguists and native speakers that aims to document every existing language and collect that knowledge into a public digital library. Even if the languages do become extinct in everyday life, they will at least have been preserved, allowing researchers to use historical written and recorded materials. Rosetta currently holds more than 70 000 pages of information on some 2500 languages. As well as an online corpus, the Rosetta Project has also been distributed to national libraries and sold to the public as a DVD.

Activity 25 (self-assessment)

How does the Rosetta Project try to guarantee the survival of languages?

The Foundation has created a version of Rosetta that can be used in the event of a disaster that renders digital data useless. The Rosetta Disk (Figure 17) is a little under 10 centimetres in diameter and contains over 13 000 pages representing over 1500 human languages.

Figure 17   The Rosetta Disk

Major languages spiral in from the outer rim; families of languages are broken down into geographic regions, with individual languages stored by micro-etching in the grid-like pattern around the picture of the Earth. A small number of disks have been created from some of the most durable materials known to science and distributed around the world, where they serve not only as valuable records but also as works of art.

Activity 26 (exploratory)

Use the information you have just read on the Long Now Foundation, and any other sources you choose, to write a short report on how the Rosetta Disk has been designed. You should write your report for an interested non-specialist audience such as an adult member of your family. You should aim to explain how and why the disk has been created and some of the techniques used to guarantee its survival into the future. Your report should be no more than 400 words, *excluding* the citations for any additional sources you use.

For this activity you should use the structure shown below:
- Title – give your report a name
- Introduction – explain the purpose of the report
- Main body – explain what you found out about the Rosetta Disk
- Conclusions – summarise the main findings in one or two sentences
- References.

To help you, a link to some information on report writing is provided in the resources page associated with this part on the TU100 website.

Comment

Below is my attempt at writing the short report. Your report will differ from mine, but I hope that you have set it out in the same way and that it makes similar points.

Report on the Rosetta Disk
1 Introduction

The aim of this report is to explain how and why the Rosetta Disk has been created. I will also describe some of the techniques used to guarantee its survival into the future.

2 The Rosetta Disk

2.1 Creation of the Rosetta Disk

The Rosetta Project began as a Long Now Foundation experiment to draw attention to the problem of digital obsolescence and to show how creative archival methods can be used to address this problem. The foundation decided to collect and archive information about human languages. The Rosetta Disk is a physical archive for the languages collected by the Rosetta Project. It is also intended to be a work of art in itself.

2.2 How was the project designed?

Inspired by the Rosetta Stone, the Rosetta Disk has at its core what it calls 'a set of parallel information', which is intended to form a key to the information we leave behind. The parallel information consists of the same texts, sets of vocabularies and descriptions for over 1500 languages. The texts include the opening chapters of the Book of Genesis and the UN Declaration on Human Rights.

2.3 Techniques to ensure longevity

The Rosetta Disk is made from nickel; it is only 3 inches in diameter, but has over 14 000 pages of information etched microscopically onto it. Each page is an image that the human eye can read by using $500 \times$ magnification. Because they are not a digital representation, the texts are not dependent on any particular format or platform. The disk is stored in a 4-inch glass and steel sphere, which should protect it from casual damage. The Long Now Foundation hopes that the disk will remain legible for thousands of years.

3 Conclusions

The Rosetta Disk is made of a durable material, nickel, and represented in a form that is platform and format independent. The disk is stored in a way that should protect it from damage. For these reasons, it is hoped that the information it contains will still be readable for thousands of years into the future.

References

Long Now Foundation (n.d.) 'About' and 'Concept', *The Rosetta Project* [online], San Francisco, CA, The Long Now Foundation, http://rosettaproject.org/about/ and http://rosettaproject.org/disk/concept/ (accessed 1 December 2010).

Wikipedia (2010) 'Rosetta Project' in *Wikipedia: the free encyclopedia* [online], http://en.wikipedia.org/wiki/Rosetta_Disk (accessed 1 December 2010).

Not content with preserving all human languages, the Long Now Foundation is planning on building a central repository for information about every computer file format that has ever been developed, and creating software to convert obsolete formats into more modern formats. This project is known as Format Exchange, and if it is ever completed it should ensure that data is never left trapped in an unreadable format and can always be put to use on a current computer. Moreover, if you visit the Long Now website you will see that years are not given in the familiar four-digit format, but a five-digit format that will only run out of numbers in the year 99999! In Long Now format, the year this document was written is 02010.

7.3 Conclusion

This session showed you two projects that are attempting to preserve data into the indefinite future. Two approaches have been taken – to make copies of data so that the loss of one record is not a catastrophic loss, and to try to make almost indestructible records.

The Wayback Machine can be thought of as a backup for the internet. Data is copied from individual servers to a remote location so that it can be preserved even if the original site changes or is deleted. The Wayback Machine can be used to examine the evolution of sites and of content, and is very useful for researchers. A complementary approach is that taken by the Long Now Foundation. Its Rosetta Disk not only holds copies of human languages, but has been manufactured from immensely durable materials that will resist the passage of time.

This session should have helped you with the following learning outcomes.

- Discuss the value of the long-term persistence of data.
- Write a short report on a technical subject after completing independent research.

Resurrecting data

8

The final session of this part of the block is given over to showing how old data can prove to be a treasure trove of new information that sometimes its creators could not have imagined. I will use a case study of a historical event that has been reinterpreted by modern technology; then, to conclude the session, I will bring the story of Domesday up to date.

8.1   Laki – old data, new threats

In this section you will explore a research project that suggests over 20 000 Britons died in a previously unknown catastrophe during the late summer of 1783. The cause was not war, famine or disease; it was a distant volcanic eruption.

Until the spring of 2010, it would not have occurred to most Britons that volcanic activity could cause any disruption to their everyday lives. That April, a relatively small volcanic eruption from Iceland's Eyjafjallajökull released a cloud of fine ash that eventually covered most of western Europe (Figure 18). The ash, invisible from the ground, posed a threat to jet airliners and resulted in the closure of much of the continent's airspace, causing billions of pounds' worth of damage. Hundreds of thousands of tonnes of sulfur spread alongside the ash; as far afield as southern Sweden and the English Midlands, people reported that the air smelt of rotten eggs.

Sulfur or sulphur?

You might have thought that this part had been written by an American, or that my editors had failed to correct a spelling mistake; but in fact, my spelling of sulfur is correct. The names of chemical elements and compounds are standardised by the International Union of Pure and Applied Chemistry (IUPAC). The US spelling was adopted as an international standard in 1990 and is now the accepted standard for both the Royal Society of Chemistry and the Qualifications and Curriculum Authority (which oversees examinations and assessment). In balance, the IUPAC also standardised the spelling of element 13 as 'aluminium' rather than the US 'aluminum'.

Figure 18   An image of the Eyjafjallajökull eruption cloud taken by the NASA Terra satellite on 15 April 2010: Iceland is located near the top left of the image behind a layer of cloud, northern Scotland is just visible at the bottom right and the western coast of Norway lies along the right-hand margin; a brown ash cloud extends from Eyjafjallajökull on Iceland's southern coast towards the bottom right of the photograph

Yet this was not the first time such volcanic plumes had reached from Icelandic volcanoes. More than two centuries earlier, an even larger eruption had made its presence felt across Europe.

> This past week, and the two prior to it, more poison fell from the sky than words can describe: ash, volcanic hairs, rain full of sulfur and saltpeter, all of it mixed with sand. The snouts, nostrils, and feet of livestock grazing or walking on the grass turned bright yellow and raw. All water went tepid and light blue in color and gravel slides turned gray. All the earth's plants burned, withered and turned gray, one after another, as the fire increased and neared the settlements.

(Steingrímsson, 1998 [1783])

Steingrímsson was the parish priest for Kirkjubæjarklaustur, a tiny town in the south-west of Iceland. Like many men of his era, he was something of an amateur scientist. His meticulous diaries are some of the first detailed, scientifically accurate reports of volcanic activity ever made and they depict some of the horror of what his parishioners were experiencing.

In June 1783, a 25 km long fissure opened in the Laki region and began to disgorge lava on a scale never seen before or since in recorded history. During fissure eruptions, lava does not pour from a crater; rather, it emerges along a long crack as a series of lava fountains and then spreads over the surrounding terrain. Figure 19 shows the 2010 fissure eruption at Fimmvörðuháls ridge in southern Iceland, which preceded the much larger Eyjafjallajökull eruption seen in Figure 18. The Fimmvörðuháls fissure was some 300 m long with four craters – yet although this is impressive, it is insignificant compared to the Laki eruption.

Figure 19   The Fimmvörðuháls fissure eruption of 2010

During the next eight months, Laki's kilometre-high fountains buried farms and pastureland under a 45 billion tonne ocean of black lava and cinder. Despite the scale of the devastation, the true disaster – the Móðuharðindin or 'Mist Hardships' – was only just beginning. The solidifying lava breathed out a sinister blue haze that eventually blanketed much of Iceland. Crops and grass withered within minutes of being exposed to the mist; animals breathing the haze sickened and died.

> The foul smell of the air, bitter as seaweed and reeking of rot for days on end, was such that many people, especially those with chest ailments, could no more than half-fill their lungs of this air, particularly if the sun was no longer in the sky; indeed, it was most astonishing that anyone should live another week.

> (Steingrímsson, ibid.)

Geologists have observed similar mists after subsequent Icelandic eruptions and we now know that the Laki fog contained two toxic gases, sulfur dioxide and hydrogen fluoride.

The mist persisted for almost two years, during which 80% of all the sheep and half of all the cattle and horses in Iceland died. The effect on the human population was almost as profound; 10 000 people, one fifth of the island's population, died from famine. The situation became so serious that the then occupying power of Denmark considered evacuating Iceland's entire population.

Beyond Iceland, volcanic ash fell on Britain throughout the summer of 1783, which became known as 'the Sand Summer'. The ash falls were accompanied by a choking yellow sulfurous fog that rolled in from the Atlantic to blanket much of western Europe, eventually spreading as far as Prague. The harvest was a disaster; there were food shortages, hunger and in some places riots. This is how Gilbert White, naturalist, described the conditions in his daily journal.

> The summer of the year 1783 was an amazing and portentous one, and full of horrible phaenomena; for, besides the alarming meteors and tremendous thunder-storms that affrighted and distressed the different counties of this kingdom, the peculiar haze, or smokey fog, that prevailed for many weeks in this island, and in every part of Europe, and even beyond its limits, was a most extraordinary appearance, unlike anything known within the memory of man. By my journal I find that I had noticed this strange occurrence from June 23 to July 20 inclusive, during which period the wind varied to every quarter without making any alteration in the air. The sun, at noon, looked as blank as a clouded moon, and shed a rust-coloured ferruginous light on the ground, and floors of rooms; but was particularly lurid and blood-coloured at rising and setting. All the time the heat was so intense that butchers' meat could hardly be eaten on the day after it was killed; and the flies swarmed so in the lanes and hedges that they rendered the horses half frantic, and riding irksome. The country people began to look with a superstitious awe at the red, louring aspect of the sun.

(White, 1789, pp. 301–2)

In 2003 John Grattan, Michael Durand and S. Taylor, three scientists from the University of Wales, Aberystwyth and the University of Canterbury, New Zealand, collaborated on a scientific paper that suggested that the half-forgotten (at least outside Iceland) Laki eruption had had a catastrophic effect on Britain and western Europe (Grattan et al., 2003). They suggested that the highly toxic gases spewing from the volcano had travelled much further than previously thought and had blanketed much of Europe in a thick acidic cloud that would have had much the same effect on human health as modern urban smog.

The result of exposing millions of people to a toxic cloud for a prolonged period of time would be an increase in the death rate amongst the population. Death rates far above normal are termed 'mortality crises' and are often associated with war, epidemic disease or crop failures. None of these conditions applied in England during 1783–1784. If England experienced a mortality crisis during that period, it must have had a previously unrecognised origin.

Death rates do not remain constant throughout the year; indeed, in rural societies (such as that of eighteenth-century England) they show a distinct seasonal variation. In the absence of a mortality crisis, deaths peak in the late winter when weather conditions are poor and food supplies limited, and reach a minimum in the late summer and early autumn with benign weather and plentiful food. Steingrímsson's records tell us that Laki was at its most violent during the summer of 1783, and it would have been during this time that the largest amount of sulfur dioxide was blown towards Europe. The poisonous gas should then have caused a sharp increase in the death rate for the summer months.

Church records from across Britain contain an invaluable record of baptisms, marriages and burials. In much of the country, uninterrupted records stretch back over five centuries – in some places even further. Long before there was a systematic national census, parish records were handwritten in a standard format and carefully stored. The single largest problem with using these records is their nature: tens of thousands of fragile books containing handwritten notes of variable quality. However, once this data has been digitised – often by the laborious process of hand-keying data into computers – it can be processed like any other. This sometimes produces new, often unsuspected information.

A mortality crisis in 1783 should be apparent in parish burial records, which provide not only the date of interment but also the age of the deceased. There are two major records holding mortality information: The Population History of England, which contains information for the whole country, and the Population History of England Database, a computerised system providing figures at a parish level. Both of these sources have been extensively verified and are regarded as providing accurate data.

The Laki theory can only be explored using computerised historical records – there is simply no way that the same work could be undertaken with paper records. The huge databases that have been built by digitising the writings of long-forgotten individuals certainly contain useful scientific data that has yet to be analysed. Climate scientists, epidemiologists and historians are increasingly using these databases to find evidence for their theories.

Activity 27 (self-assessment)

If much of England experienced pollution from Laki, what would you expect to see in the mortality records?

The possibility that Laki was responsible for thousands of deaths in the UK and the remainder of western Europe remains controversial. However, if the theory is true, it is worth remembering that Iceland is one of the most volcanically active places on Earth; the Laki eruption was just one of many that have occurred on the island, and will occur again.

Activity 28 (exploratory)

In this activity you are going to use Google Apps to perform some statistical analysis of the English burial records for the eighteenth century. At the end of the activity you will produce a short report on your work. When convenient, go to the resources page associated with this part on the TU100 website and find the instructions for this activity.

8.2   Emulating the past

In cases where computer hardware is no longer available, it is possible to write an *emulator*: a program that replicates the operation of a physical computer in software. The heart of an emulator is a *virtual machine* – a computer program that translates commands written for the machine being emulated into commands understood by the host computer.

Virtual machines are widely used in computer programming. For instance, the Sense programming environment runs in a virtual machine belonging to the Squeak language. Squeak virtual machines exist for most common computers, meaning that a single Squeak program can be run on a range of computers. As another example, Sun Microsystems' Java programming language is the most widespread virtual machine in the world. Although the idea was not invented at Sun, it became popular through Java's advertising slogan 'write once, run anywhere'. Such is the flexibility of the Java virtual machine that the same program can be run on devices as diverse as supercomputers, mobile phones and even smart cards.

Virtual machines may sound like the solution to running software designed for obsolete computers, but there are penalties:

- programs running on a virtual machine run relatively slowly compared to programs executing on the original hardware
- virtual machines use relatively large amounts of memory, since the computer must store the virtual machine as well as the program being executed.

Fortunately, computers have advanced so rapidly that it is possible for virtual machines to emulate older computers on even quite modest PCs. Emulators exist for many of the most famous historic computers, including Colossus and the Manchester Baby, as well as many of the pioneering microcomputers of the 1980s and a wide variety of video game consoles.

Emulation and the law

Many emulations may be illegal. Almost all computer hardware and software is given legal protection by a set of principles known as *intellectual property (IP)* – which should not be confused with the abbreviation for Internet Protocol. Very simply, these principles restrict the rights of others to copy, distribute or alter a piece of work. Intellectual property remains in place even after a product is removed from sale, the original company ceases trading or the death of the authors.

You will learn more about intellectual property in the next part of this block.

When companies merge, intellectual property is transferred to the new owners. Over a number of years it can change hands many times. To give a relatively simple example, the ZX Spectrum was one of the most popular microcomputers in the UK throughout the 1980s (Figure 20). Introduced in 1982 and costing £175, it was the first relatively cheap colour computer available in the UK and was sold through high-street stores. During its ten-year lifespan over 20 000 software titles were published for the Spectrum, and it is widely credited with giving birth to the UK's world-class video games industry. Yet although the Spectrum was developed by Sinclair Research, its intellectual property was transferred to Amstrad when Sinclair Research was sold. Amstrad continues to hold all the rights to the Spectrum intellectual property, even though production of the Spectrum was discontinued in 1992.

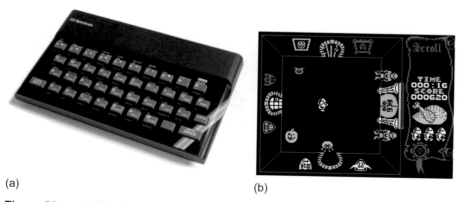

(a)   (b)

Figure 20 **(a) The Sinclair ZX Spectrum; (b)** *Atic Atac,* **one of the Spectrum's most famous games, being emulated in software on an Apple Macintosh**

It can be very hard to determine who owns a particular piece of intellectual property, but the authors of emulators are obliged to attempt to obtain permission from the intellectual property holder before they can develop their emulation. If they fail to do so, the intellectual property holder can take legal action for damages and to have the emulator removed from distribution.

In extreme cases a company might cease trading or an author may die without the intellectual property being transferred to a new holder, in which case the product is said to be an *orphan*. Technically the product is still protected by intellectual property, but developers may not be able to obtain legal permission to use the work. Many countries are grappling with the issue of orphaned products (which also include books, music and films), but it will be many years before it can be resolved.

8.3 Return to Domesday

Only 15 years after being created at enormous expense, the BBC Domesday Project was, to all intents and purposes, useless. The hardware and software had long since been supplanted by modern technologies, and it appeared that the huge amount of data collected would be lost forever.

However, Domesday was about to be reborn.

Sally Pearce, a senior lecturer at the University of Brighton, had been one of the volunteers who spent 1984 collecting information for the project. She even had two of the precious Laservision discs that had been used by the university. Sally asked her husband Adrian – an experienced computer engineer – if the Domesday Project could be ported to modern PCs. The only way to answer that question was to find out how the Domesday Project had originally worked.

Adrian obtained one of the surprisingly rare BBC Master computers and, after spending time restoring it to working condition, took it upon himself to learn exactly how the machine had been designed and worked. He was then able to find a working LV-ROM Laservision player and make a suitable cable to connect it to the BBC computer. The BBC Master was in turn connected to a PC that would store data on its hard disk. When Adrian put the Laservision disc into the player, he was able to (extremely slowly) extract data from the Domesday archive and save it onto the PC. Figure 21 shows Adrian holding in his right hand one of the 30 cm Laservision discs used to store Domesday data; a modern CD is in the foreground for comparison.

Adrian was able to recover over 300 MB of data, including text and raw hexadecimal data as well as the compiled programs that had once controlled the Domesday program. Not only had the programs been written in an obsolete programming language called BCPL, with which Adrian was unfamiliar, but he only had the compiled (machine-readable) versions – not the human-readable source code. However, Adrian was gradually able to unpick the whole structure of the Domesday discs; most importantly, he was able to replicate the search program that allowed users to find any information on the disc.

Figure 21 Adrian Pearce, the first person to recover information from the BBC Domesday Project

Although Adrian had recovered the text and programs on the disc, he had not been able to restore the videos and still images, which had been stored in a long-abandoned format. Adrian attempted to obtain the images using a plug-in PC card called a frame grabber, which copies images from video memory. However, frame grabbing is extremely time-consuming and the images tend to be of much poorer quality than the originals.

Fortunately, Adrian wasn't the only person working on Domesday. In 2002, the National Archives had founded the Digital Preservation Coalition, a group of researchers dedicated to preserving digital data for future generations. Andy Finney, who had originally worked on the Domesday Project, had located the original analogue video tapes used to store all the images and video for the discs. The BBC had also retained some of the original analogue tape drives in their own archives and agreed to transfer the contents of the tapes onto digital tape format, which would at least conserve their contents for a few more years. At the same time, the images were converted into standard JPEG images that could be displayed on any PC.

The entire Domesday Project has now been conserved and is on public display at the National Archives in Kew, London. Sadly, Adrian died shortly after the project was completed and this has resulted in problems with making the archive more widely available. Hopefully, these issues will be resolved in the near future and Domesday will be published on the Web.

8.4   Conclusion

This session covered some of the uses that historical data can be put to. Computers allow enormous amounts of historical data to be processed in reasonable amounts of time. Computer analysis of digitised parish records from England was used to show the changes in mortality during the eighteenth century, revealing a previously unidentified increase in the death rate that might have been caused by airborne pollution from a volcanic eruption.

You also explored the role of emulation in recreating lost technologies. Software emulation of outdated computer hardware allows developers to continue to run applications designed for these computers, or to access data held in obsolete formats.

Finally you saw an alternative to emulation, which is to port data from an older platform to a newer one – but as you saw from Adrian Pearce's experiences with the BBC Domesday Project, this is an extremely laborious task.

This session should have helped you with the following learning outcomes.

- Explain the role of emulation in preserving computer data.
- Give examples of data recovery from historical sources.
- Perform statistical analysis to identify trends in data.

Summary

This part gave you an insight into the concept of data having a lifetime. You have learned that data is surprisingly fragile; it can degrade or be lost entirely, either because of deterioration in the medium on which it is stored or through technological or cultural changes that make it unreadable.

Physical deterioration can be prevented by regularly making copies of the data onto a fresh medium. This part showed that various types of media have widely differing characteristics such as speed, reliability and lifetime, and these affect their suitability for backing up data. You should now be able to identify a suitable backup strategy for your own computer use.

This part also demonstrated that although data may apparently be lost by activities such as the formatting of a disk, in reality the data remains recoverable. You learned how sophisticated software tools can recover apparently deleted data during forensic investigations, and how data can be deleted once and for all.

The effects of technological and cultural changes can be minimised by the creation and imposition of technological standards. You learned that these standards can arise in an ad hoc manner or through a formal standardisation process. As well as helping to ensure that data remains readable into the future, standards also help to drive down the cost of hardware and software alike.

Finally you learned about the preservation and use of historical data. I used the Wayback Machine as an example of a resource where web pages can be archived for the indefinite future. You also had an opportunity to perform some statistical analysis on historical population data stored in the Population History of England Database.

Once you have completed all the online activities associated with this part and investigated the resources associated with it, you can move on to Part 5, which directly follows this part in the book. The last part of Block 3, it will introduce you to the open source movement and how it is being extended beyond software development.

Answers to self-assessment activities

Activity 2

The book was written on long-lasting parchment using permanent ink, so the medium was important. It was then kept in a safe box in a secure location and only opened on rare occasions – so storage was also important. The book was written in a language (Latin) that is still understood and has not changed since the book was written; this use of a common language kept the document useful.

Activity 4

I came up with the following (you might have thought of others).

- *Memory chips*: SD and Compact Flash cards, USB flash drives, video game consoles, smart cards, solid-state drives (SSDs) and the built-in memory found in devices such as media players and cheap video cameras.
- *Optical media*: compact discs and CD-recordable, DVD and DVD-recordable formats, Blu-ray and Blu-ray recordable formats, HD-DVD, UMD and Laserdisc.
- *Magnetic media*: hard disks, floppy disks, magnetic tape (audio, video and data formats).

Activity 5

I feel they all apply to me, although clearly some (such as losing a disk) are more likely than others (such as terrorism).

Activity 6

Regular copies are needed to prevent the data being affected by any deterioration in the storage medium. Multiple copies are required to insure against the loss or damage of any one piece of data.

Activity 10

JournalSpace could have written the data to optical discs, tapes or hard disks that were then placed in a safe store, or they could have used an offsite backup service. However, in both cases the data could still have been destroyed if the guilty employee had access to the data store or to the offsite backups. System administrators who have access to data and backups must be not only highly trained, but also impeccably honest.

Activity 11

The messages were thought to be unimportant and a waste of valuable backup capacity.

Activity 12

(a) In this case the user could open the Recycle Bin and drag the file out (or right-click on the file in the Bin and choose Restore).

(b) Here the user would have to use an undelete program.

Activity 13

They should *immediately* stop using the computer and try to recover the data using an undelete utility. The less time that elapses between deleting the file and trying to undelete it, the less chance there has been for that part of the disk to be overwritten.

Activity 14

Absolutely not. Installing the application will write files to the disk that could overwrite the deleted data. Almost all undelete applications can be run either from CD or from a removable USB flash drive.

Activity 16

A unique hash value is associated with the files and their arrangement on a hard disk. Any changes to the hard disk's contents reveal themselves because they produce a new hash. Investigators can be confident that their copy of the disk is identical to the original by comparing their own independently generated hash with that supplied by the organisation holding the original disk.

Activity 20

1 Developers who use the PDF format are more likely to use Adobe's expensive professional tools such as Photoshop, Illustrator and Acrobat.

2 Because PDF is now an open standard, there is no reason for rival companies to develop their own proprietary format in competition with PDF.

Activity 21

Any software developer could now support the format in their products without seeking (or paying for) a licence from Microsoft.

Activity 22

- The PC used an open architecture, making it possible for other companies to build components that could be slotted into the computer, or write software for the PC, without paying licence fees.

- The reference manual was also open as it gave detailed technical information about the workings of the machine.

- The BIOS was proprietary – the executable programs were not made public.

Activity 23

The three key decisions were:

1 using off-the-shelf components wherever possible

2 using an open architecture

3 publishing the specifications in a publicly available reference manual.

Activity 25

It collects the languages into a digital library that can be accessed by anyone. The library is made available online, but also distributed (to improve its survivability) through national libraries and on DVD.

Activity 27

The records would show a mortality crisis with sharply increased burial rates. If the crisis was a national event, the death rate would increase across the whole of the country at more or less the same time.

Glossary

accelerated ageing   A testing method that aims to determine the lifespan of a product when actual data is unavailable (usually because the product contains novel technologies or materials).

archive   A collection of documents or set of data that will be retained unchanged for future use.

array   In hardware, a collection of disks that together form a RAID.

backup   A copy of data held on a computer system. Backups record the state of a computer system at a given time and are designed to protect against data loss or a catastrophic failure. Full backups copy all the data on a machine, whilst incremental backups copy only data that has changed since the last backup.

backwards compatibility   The ability of a modern device or technology to meaningfully receive an input designed for older devices.

clean room design   The process of producing a functionally identical copy of a piece of hardware or software without copying the original item. The process is used to circumvent intellectual property laws and to avoid paying licensing fees to the holder of the original technologies. Also known as *Chinese wall design*.

data remanence   Data remaining on a storage device despite supposedly having been deleted or erased.

defrag   An operating system process for organising the physical location of files on a disk. As a disk is used, files are broken into fragments that can be scattered over the surface of the disk; such fragmentation increases the amount of time taken to read files as well as increasing wear and tear on the device. Defragmentation joins file fragments together and attempts to locate related files close together on the disk.

degaussing   The process of applying a strong magnetic field to a magnetic storage device in order to erase any information held on that device.

Digital Dark Age   In a technological context, a possible future society where it is impossible to read historical records, either because they have been stored in an obsolete format or because the material used to hold the data has deteriorated beyond use.

digital obsolescence   The process of digital media becoming unreadable because the physical medium – the device required to read the media, whether it is the hardware or the software that runs on it – is no longer available. Digital obsolescence is a form of technological obsolescence.

disruptive technology   A product or service whose introduction displaces an existing product or service.

emulator   A program that imitates the functions of one computer or operating system on another computer. Emulation is a way of overcoming digital obsolescence.

forensic computing   A branch of forensic science that is concerned with obtaining legal evidence from computer systems. Also known as *computer forensics* or *digital forensics*.

format   To prepare a computer storage device for use. Any data previously held on the device is made unavailable to the operating system and the device appears empty. It may be possible to recover this data using specialised forensic software.

fragmentation   An unwanted process in which computer files are split across a number of locations on a disk as the disk becomes full. Fragmentation slows down file access and increases wear and tear on the disk drive itself. Some operating systems automatically defragment files when idling; others require the user to run special defragmentation programs.

hash   A unique identifier for a piece of information. Hashes are fixed-sized pieces of data generated from arbitrarily large files using mathematical processes. They are used to authenticate data in many security applications, as well as being used to speed up access to very large databases.

image   A single file containing the complete contents and structure of a storage device (such as a disk). Disk images are often used for distributing very large programs (especially on the Apple Macintosh), or used to replicate a disk for forensic purposes.

imaging   The process of creating an image file.

linear access format   A type of storage where data is sequentially written to a medium such as magnetic tape or paper tape. Later records are written at the end of existing records and require a greater amount of time to access. Linear access is relatively simple to develop, but suffers from the drawback that it is slow to access or write data since it is necessary to fast-forward or rewind through other records. As well as data storage, linear access is also used for audio and video tape. Also known as *sequential access format*.

migrate   To move data from one medium to another to ensure it remains readable.

open format   A published specification for storing data that can be used by anyone. The specification may be managed by a standards body such as ISO. If there is no charge for using an open format then it is called a free file format. See also **proprietary format**.

orphan   (1) A computer product or technology that has been abandoned by its original developers. An orphaned technology is still protected by intellectual property laws such as copyright, trademarks and patents, even if it is not actively sold or supported. Orphaned technologies are sometimes called 'abandonware'. (2) A piece of work such as a book, musical composition, photograph, film or game whose copyright holder cannot be determined.

overwriting   The process of obscuring sensitive information that might remain on a disk before disposal. New data, usually just all zeros or all ones but sometimes a random pattern of both, is written to every part of the disk. This is a time-consuming process, especially if multiple overwrites are used. Also known as *wiping* or *shredding*.

port   To adapt software so that it can be used on a completely different computer architecture or operating system from the one for which it was originally designed.

proprietary format   A specification for storing data that remains under the control of a private body such as a company. Other developers may use a proprietary format only after agreeing to licensing terms and usually paying for the licence. See also **open format**.

random access format   A type of computer storage that allows files to be accessed in any order within a certain amount of time. Random access is used to store data in computer memory and on magnetic and optical discs. Also known as *direct access format*.

Redundant Array of Inexpensive Disks (RAID)   A method of improving the reliability of disk storage by storing data on more than one disk; the collection of disks form an array that appears as a single device to a computer.

standard   In general, an agreed specification for doing something. In the context of TU100, a standard is an agreed specification for the way in which components of a system will operate and interact with each other.

technological obsolescence   The process by which existing technologies cease to be used when they are displaced by new technologies.

undelete   To recover a deleted file from a disk. Undelete facilities are not offered by some operating systems; in such cases, files can be retrieved only by using specialised data recovery programs.

virtual machine   A computer program that simulates the execution of a program on a physical computer.

References

BBC News (2009) 'Air France 'black box' hunt ends', *BBC News* [online], 20 August, http://news.bbc.co.uk/1/hi/world/europe/8212569.stm (accessed 1 December 2010).

Berners-Lee, T. (1991) 'WorldWideWeb: Summary', post to discussion in alt.hypertext newsgroup, Usenet, 6 August.

Cabbage, M. and Harwood, W. (2004) *Comm Check... The Final Flight of Shuttle Columbia*, New York, Free Press.

Grattan, J., Durand, M. and Taylor, S. (2003) 'Illness and elevated human mortality in Europe coincident with the Laki fissure eruption' in Oppenheimer, C., Pyle, D.M. and Barclay, J. (eds) *Volcanic Degassing*, Special Publication 213, London, Geological Society.

Steingrímsson, J. (1998 [1783]) *Fires of the Earth: The Laki Eruption, 1783–1784*, Reykjavík, Nordic Volcanological Institute and University of Iceland Press.

The X Lab (n.d.) *Optical media longevity* [online], The X Lab, http://www.thexlab.com/faqs/opticalmedialongevity.html (accessed 1 December 2010).

White, G. (1789) *The Natural History and Antiquities of Selborne*, London, B. White and Son.

ZDNet (2002) 'Tech Guide: Storage media lifespans', *ZDNet* [online], 14 October, http://www.zdnet.com.au/tech-guide-storage-media-lifespans-120269043.htm (accessed 1 December 2010).

Acknowledgements

Grateful acknowledgement is made to the following sources.

Figures

Figures 1 and 2: © The National Archives

Figures 3(a) and 3(b): Courtesy of IBM UK

Figure 4: © CERN Geneva

Figure 5: © Data Robotics Inc.

Figure 6: Courtesy of Iomega Corporation

Figure 17: Courtesy of Rolfe Horn and www.longnow.org

Figure 18: NASA image by Jeff Schmaltz, MODIS Rapid Response Team at NASA GSFC

Figure 19: © iStockphoto.com/Enrique Pedrero Pachero

Figure 20(a): Bill Bertram, www.flickr.com, used under http://en.wikipedia.org/wiki/Creative_Commons

Figure 20(b): Taken from http://opensourcezx.untergrund.net

Figure 21: Taken from www.ariadne.ac.uk

Every effort has been made to contact copyright holders. If any have been inadvertently overlooked the publishers will be pleased to make the necessary arrangements at the first opportunity.

Part 5

Giving it all away

Author: Tony Nixon

Introduction

I wrote the first draft of this part of TU100 in an application called Open Office. The application cost me nothing to obtain (except a little time to download) and I didn't have to pay a licence fee. It contains virtually all of the facilities of similar applications, such as Microsoft Office, for which I would have to pay. Indeed, a user of Microsoft Office would not find Open Office at all difficult to use for most word processing or spreadsheet work, and he or she could easily exchange documents with a Microsoft Office user without too many compatibility problems.

Open Office has existed since October 2000 as an *open source* project. OpenOffice.org 1.0, the product that emerged from that project, was released in April 2002. As you will see, it is by no means the first open source project, but it is one of the most popular. In addition, I am running Open Office on a computer using an operating system called Ubuntu for which, again, I didn't have to pay a fee. Ubuntu, which you read a little about in Part 2 of this block, is based on an open source operating system called Linux (or, more precisely, GNU-Linux).

So, you might ask, given that the software is free and will do the job, why isn't everybody using it? Why would anyone choose to pay? Also, and perhaps more interestingly, what motivates organisations and individuals to contribute to software that is free? Finally, and perhaps most important of all, is it any good?

This part of TU100 is about open source, not only in the context of software projects but also as a movement that departs from traditional business models. In it I will address the questions above, as well as describing the origins of the open source software movement and identifying ways in which this model is being extended beyond software development.

Many of the recent developments in ubiquitous computing have been driven by open source software. For example, Android and Symbian are open source operating systems found in many popular mobile devices, such as smart phones and handheld computers. Open source methods extend beyond the world of software to hardware such as your Arduino board (which is a part of the hardware you use with Sense) and Sun SPOT (a Sun Microsystems programmable device of a similar nature). As you will see in the final session, the approach taken by the software developer community has even found its way into a vast range of other commodities – from automobiles to drugs.

I'd like to start by drawing your attention to the significance of open source software in the day-to-day world.

Activity 1 (exploratory)

(a) When did you last use a computer running Linux?

(b) When did you last use Google?

Comment

(a) You might have responded 'never' or 'several weeks ago'. Alternatively, if you remembered Block 1 Part 2, where you were asked how many computers you used in one day, you might have been a little bit more wary.

(b) My point here is simply to remind you that Google uses servers that run on a Linux operating system.

Netcraft is an internet services company that provides a facility to identify which operating systems are currently in use for a given *domain*. The screenshot in Figure 1 was taken from a search using Netcraft in 2010. I selected microsoft.com as the domain of interest. As you can see, most of the servers are running either unknown operating systems or (as you might expect) Microsoft Windows 2003 and 2008, but two on this page are running Linux. You might find this result surprising given the nature of Microsoft's business.

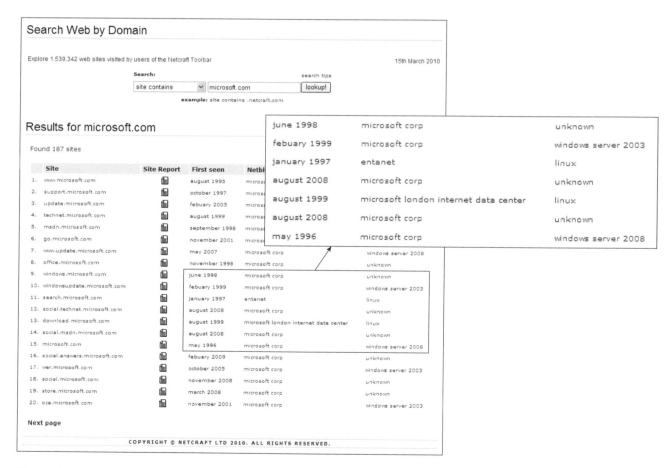

Figure 1   Screenshot from Netcraft showing operating systems for Microsoft.com servers

Activity 2 (exploratory)

When convenient, go online and use Netcraft to look at some of your favourite websites to see which operating systems they use. For example, you might wish to try the following domains: google.com, amazon.com and channel4.co.uk. The link you need is provided in the resources page associated with this part on the TU100 website.

Comment

When I looked at the three domains listed above in late 2010, I found that the vast majority of their servers were running Linux.

The message here is a simple one. Linux is an open source product and it is used so widely as an operating system that even companies that manufacture operating systems (such as Microsoft) make use of it. So, what is so special about Linux and does it owe its popularity to the fact that it is open source? The simple answer is that it is extremely reliable and, yes, this is in no small part due to the fact that it is open source.

To summarise, this part of TU100 is about open source:

- what it is
- how it came to be
- how it is developed
- how it relates to business
- how it goes beyond software.

I hope you enjoy studying it.

97

Learning outcomes

Your study of this part will help you to do the following.

Knowledge and understanding

- Describe the difference between source code and machine code.
- Understand the basic principles behind patents, trademarks and copyright.
- Explain the purpose of licensing.
- Name and give a brief history of some important open source projects.
- Describe what constitutes a system.
- Explain how it is possible to develop business models from open source initiatives.
- Describe a simple model for open source development.

Cognitive skills

- Relate different business models that are based around open source.
- Identify where it may be possible to extend open source methods.

Key skills

- Develop skills in working with diagrams.

Background to open source

In this first session I want to give you some of the background information that will help you to understand what open source is. I will start by looking at what the term 'open source' means, before considering some of the legal concepts that underlie the principles of open source – patents, trademarks and copyright. I will then go on to look at licensing, in preparation for introducing you to some different kinds of licence later in the part.

1.1 Why call it 'open source'?

The term *open source* refers to the original code from which a piece of software is developed. This is called the *source code*. As you have seen when writing programs in Sense, once you understand the basics of using a programming language, it is not difficult to modify or even write a piece of software from scratch. But, as you learned in Block 2 Part 1, the code that is actually used by the computer is translated from the high-level language in which it was originally written into a binary code that the computer understands. We call this *machine language* or *machine code*. Figure 2 shows a simple program as source code and as machine code. I hope that you can see that the source code is much more readable than the machine code.

```
/**
 * Simple HelloButton() method.
 * @version 1.0
 * @author john doe <doe.j@example.com>
 */
HelloButton()
{
  JButton hello = new JButton( "Hello, wor
  hello.addActionListener( new HelloBtnList

  // use the JFrame type until support for t
  // new component is finished
  JFrame frame = new JFrame( "Hello Button"
  Container pane = frame.getContentPane();
  pane.add( hello );
  frame.pack();

} frame.show();          // display the fra
```

```
1000111000111001 0000010001111100
1000010111110011 1000100010111011
1000010111011110 0010111101100010
1110000101000111 1111000001110111
0011101110011100 1110000111001111
1000111000111001 0000010001111100
1100010110110011 1000101010111011
0000010111011110 0010110101100010
0110000101000101 1111000001110011
0011101110011100 1110010111001111
```

Figure 2 **Source code (left) is easier to read and to modify than machine code (right)**

The source code is rarely provided alongside a piece of software; only the machine code (for use by the computer) is supplied. Even if the source code were made available, or we could somehow modify the machine code in a meaningful way, the *rights* to the software would be owned by someone or some organisation, so we would usually be forbidden under the licence agreement from making alterations. The term 'open source' refers to providing access to the source code as well as licensing the end user to make alterations.

Activity 3 (self-assessment)

Based on what you have learned from the text above, identify two ways in which you could be prevented from modifying a program on your computer.

So there are two aspects to modifying a program: I need the source code and I need permission from the owner of the software. But how does one 'own' something like software? The simple answer is through copyright – understanding the nature of copyright and licensing is key to understanding open source. So, before going further, we need to explore copyright and licensing a little. This is a complex subject, but a very basic understanding of terms such as copyright, licensing, trademarks and patents will go a long way towards helping you grasp the nature of open source projects.

1.2   Who owns what and how?

In this section you will learn a little about the legal protections given to information and ideas. This area of the law is known as *intellectual property*, and it is a huge, complicated and very profitable legal minefield. Fortunately, this is not a law course!

There are three broad areas of intellectual property law, dealing with patents, trademarks and copyright respectively. Before I discuss these, it's worth pointing out that the UK Intellectual Property Office runs an excellent website covering these subjects. You will find a link to this in the resources page associated with this part on the TU100 website.

Patents

A *patent* is a form of protection given to the creator of a piece of work that grants him or her exclusive rights to produce that work for a limited period of time; in exchange, the creator makes public the design and workings of the item. If an item is to be patented, it must be judged original and not an obvious development of an existing idea. These decisions are made by national or international patent authorities (sometimes called patent offices).

There are differences between countries as to what they allow to be patented; most patents are awarded for industrial processes and machineries, but they have also been awarded for novel plant breeds, genes and business models. One crucial difference between patent regimes is that the USA allows software to be patented, whereas (at least in theory) European countries do not currently permit this. Having said this, about 15% of European patent applications are software-related.

Incidentally, it is quite common practice for a company to file a patent simply to protect against someone else filing the same patent and in this way preventing the company from using its own idea.

Trademarks

Companies are normally very jealous of their brand identification: they see this as key to establishing and maintaining a loyal customer base, to building a reputation (for example for quality, value for money or leading fashion) and to public recognition. Name-brand advertising began in the nineteenth century in response to widespread adulteration of foodstuffs: companies fought to establish their brand as 'pure'. Since then brand names have been extended to all manner of goods and items, including the names of characters in books and films.

Rights to a brand name or a designating symbol (logo) or phrase are established through the so-called *trademark*, which is a legal term meaning that a name, symbol or phrase is registered as belonging to a particular company and cannot legally be used by any other. Trademarks have to be registered, renewed and defended in law – if they are not, the trademark is deemed to have lapsed and the name, symbol or phrase can be used by anyone. Thus companies spend large sums registering, enforcing and defending their trademarks from competitors. A trademark is indicated with either the ^{TM} or the $^{®}$ symbol; the latter shows that a trademark has been registered with a government body and offers additional protection in the event of a legal dispute. Figure 3 shows a few examples of trademarks.

Some examples of former trademarks that we use every day are petrol, yo-yo, escalator and aspirin.

Figure 3   Most of the trademarks here are instantly recognisable

Activity 4 (exploratory)

Spend no more than five minutes looking for trademarks on items in your house or office. You will often find details of the mark in the small print of manuals and on the cases of DVDs and CDs, or even printed on the bottom of items themselves. If you're stuck, try looking at the wrapping on food items such as breakfast cereals. Why do you think there are quite so many ^{TM} and ® symbols?

Comment

I'm always surprised by the number of ^{TM} and ® symbols that can be found on items – especially toys and games based on television programmes or films. The reason for their abundance is that the trademark holder must always defend their mark. If the product appeared without the appropriate symbol then it could be considered that the mark was not being actively protected, in which case a rival company might attempt to start using the mark on its own products.

Copyright

One important intellectual property concept is that of *copyright*, which originated in the UK in the early eighteenth century. Under copyright law, the creator of a piece of work is given the exclusive right to benefit from their work for a set period of time, after which the work is made freely available to all (i.e. it enters the *public domain*). Having said that, it is worth pointing out that this period of time is frequently altered because of changes to the law, so it is often the case that many significant works never reach the public domain. Copyright was designed to benefit all members of society – the creator would be rewarded for their work by being able to charge for copies in the knowledge that no one else could do likewise, whilst the rest of society would benefit by having access to the work when the copyright period expired.

Copyright can be applied to any intellectual or artistic work that has been realised in some form. A partial list of such works includes books, poems, plays, films, dances, musical scores, audio recordings, paintings, drawings, sculptures, photographs, software, radio and television broadcasts, and industrial designs. Crucially, ideas that have not been realised cannot be copyrighted. In fact it is not possible to copyright an idea; what is copyrighted is the expression of that idea.

Activity 5 (self-assessment)

Which of the following can be copyrighted? A comic book, an Open University podcast, an abstract painting, the design of a car.

The copyright symbol – © – is often used by large companies to assert their ownership of materials. It is not necessary to use this symbol to claim copyright over an item, so you cannot assume that an item is not protected by copyright just because the symbol is absent.

The 1710 UK law that created the concept of copyright dictated that works would be protected for 14 years from the date of publication. After that the author could apply for a copyright extension for a further 14 years, but in no circumstances could the copyright term extend beyond 28 years. Since then, however, there has been an inexorable increase in the length of copyright protection. In addition, copyright terms in the UK are almost uniquely complicated: rather than adopt a single period of copyright, the Copyright, Designs and Patents Act (1988) lays down a series of copyright terms for different media that depend on the type of media, the date of publication and the country of origin. Broadly, they are as follows:

- for *typographical arrangements* (such as one of your TU100 printed books), the term is 25 years from the date of publication
- broadcast material (such as television or radio programmes) created in the UK is protected for 50 years from the date of first broadcast (although, currently, there is ongoing work on a treaty to change this)
- audio materials are copyrighted for 50 years from the time they were first recorded, although this seems set to change to 70 years based on a 2009 EU directive
- copyright for the composition of dramatic works such as novels, music, art or plays lasts for 70 years after the death of the author. If more than one person was responsible, the 70-year period extends from the time of death of the last creator.

Note in all this that there is a difference between the original *composition* of a work (a novel, piece of music, etc.) and the individual *recordings* of that work (a particular typographical arrangement or audio recording). Both are subject to copyright, but in different ways.

Activity 6 (exploratory)

(a) Is this text protected by copyright?

(b) When will the copyright expire on the Beatles' original recording of their song 'Yellow Submarine' (released in 1966)?

(c) When will the copyright expire on the song 'Yellow Submarine', which was written by Paul McCartney and John Lennon?

(d) *Bleak House* by Charles Dickens was published in 1853. Is the original text still under copyright?

Comment

(a) Yes, it is. You can find the copyright notice on page 2, just after the title page.

(b) Assuming there are no changes to copyright law in the UK, the copyright on the song will expire 50 years after the recording, i.e. 1966 + 50 years = 2016.

(c) It's too early to say. At the time of writing, the copyright (in the UK) on the song will last for 70 years from the death of the last surviving author, but there is always pressure to extend copyrights and it is quite likely that the law will be changed. However, at the time of writing, Paul McCartney is still alive and well and 'Yellow Submarine' remains firmly under copyright.

(d) No. The text of *Bleak House* is in the public domain. Even if the current legislation had been in force at the time of Charles Dickens' death in 1870, the text would have entered the public domain 70 years later in 1940. Copyright for new editions (to be precise, new typographical arrangements) of the book will be granted to the publisher and will extend for 25 years from the publication date of the new edition. Significantly, this is a non-exclusive copyright; individuals can continue to access the original text of *Bleak House*, and other publishers may print their own editions of the book (for which they too will be granted copyright for that particular typographical arrangement).

Unlike patents and trademarks, copyright is an automatic right given to the creator of any suitable material; it is not granted by an outside body. In most cases, anything you create is your copyright; however, if you are contracted to produce material – for instance, as part of your job – then copyright is usually transferred to your employer.

Activity 7 (self-assessment)

Why do you think The Open University has the copyright on this text rather than the author?

In 2009, the European Union Commission extended the copyright term on sound recordings for commercial businesses from 50 years to 95 years from the date of the first recording. At the time musicians and record companies claimed that the copyright protection offered to performers was poor in comparison to that offered in the USA, where recordings are protected for 70 years beyond the death of the performer.

Once the copyright period has passed, items are said to belong in the public domain. Anyone can use and adapt those works as they see fit. Alternatively, an author of a document can choose to waive copyright at the time of publication (or any time after) and put their work in the public domain. Once an item has entered the public domain, it cannot be returned to copyright status.

Activity 8 (self-assessment)

In 2006, the BBC broadcast a highly regarded version of Charles Dickens' *Bleak House*. Is this television programme copyrighted?

Exceptionally, in the UK the King James Bible (originally printed in 1611) is protected by an indefinite Crown Copyright. Very few other publications have this status.

Activity 9 (exploratory)

Do you think long copyright terms are a good idea? Try to think of one reason why copyright should extend for a long time, and one reason why terms should be short. Spend no more than ten minutes on this exercise.

Comment

One justification for long copyright terms is that many creators produce only a handful of works in their lifetime and therefore need a long term to generate income. Having said this, however, ownership of copyright doesn't necessarily translate into a lifetime flow of ready cash; in practice the commercial life of most works is very short. In fact, before the US copyright reforms of the 1970s, most copyright owners didn't bother to renew the registration of their copyrights after 28 years (as they were required to do at the time in order to retain the copyrights).

A justification for short terms is that copyright was originally designed to enrich society. Items would enter the public domain, where they could be used by anyone; it was hoped that this would create a more literate, better educated and richer society. In fact, this idea of copyright was considered so important that it was included in the United States Constitution. Short terms mean that good ideas are spread more quickly, whilst lengthy copyright terms prevent them from being shared with society.

1.3 Licensing

Almost any software package that you acquire will have a licence agreement associated with it. You generally see this in the form of an *end-user licence agreement (EULA)* when you are asked to accept the terms and conditions by ticking a box at some point during the installation process. Licences are mechanisms for giving permission. For instance, think about a driving licence: this gives you permission to drive on public roads. From a software perspective you can regard the licence as being a contract between the owner of the copyright and the end user. The copyright enables software providers to protect the software as their property, whilst the licence gives permission for others to use it. To be in breach of a licence agreement is usually to be in breach of contract and therefore potentially liable. You might not think so from reading one, but the purpose of the EULA is to enable both parties to be clear as to their rights.

This is true not just of software but of many other products too. For example, if you purchase a film on DVD then this gives you a licence to watch that film, but usually there are a large number of things that you are restricted from doing (such as making copies or showing to large audiences outside your own home).

It is worth noting that you probably don't *own* any of the software on your computer; what you pay for are licences granted by the owners to give you permission to use it. For example, the copyright for the Windows operating system belongs to Microsoft.

Activity 10 (exploratory)

Find the EULA for your operating system.

Comment

If you are using Windows then you can find your licence agreement in a number of ways. Probably the simplest is to hit the F1 key when looking at your Windows desktop, then type license agreement (note the US spelling) or EULA into the search box. If you have difficulty finding the EULA for your operating system, ask for help in your tutor-group forum.

Here's a snippet from my Windows XP EULA:

```
1.1  Installation and use.  You may install, use, access,
     display and run one copy of the Software on a single
     computer, such as a workstation, terminal or other
     device ("Workstation Computer"). The Software may not
     be used by more than two (2) processors at any one
     time on any single Workstation Computer.
```

Even in these few lines, I think you can see the nature of licence agreements. The language is of the form 'you may ...' or 'you may not ...'; it tells me what I can and cannot do with the product.

Activity 11 (self-assessment)

In a single sentence, describe the purpose of a licence agreement.

1.4   Conclusion

This part of TU100 is about allowing people to build freely on the work of others without constraint. You might suppose that this makes copyright and licensing unnecessary, but in fact the situation is quite the reverse. Even open source products require protection and, as you will see in the next session, those who started the movement realised this from the outset.

This session should have helped you with the following learning outcomes.

- Describe the difference between source code and machine code.
- Understand the basic principles behind patents, trademarks and copyright.
- Explain the purpose of licensing.

2 The origins of open source software

Now that you've got some understanding of the principles behind copyright and licensing, I want to return to open source and look at how the first open source projects came into being. This will include short histories of some of the most successful open source projects – GNU, Linux, Firefox and Apache – as well as some of the people behind them. You will see how the concepts that you met in the previous session are just as relevant to open source products as they are to commercial products.

2.1 An angry man

To understand the origins of open source projects, we need to look back to the early 1980s and the development of something called the GNU project. GNU (a *recursive acronym* for Gnu's Not Unix, pronounced 'Guh-new') was initiated by a US programmer – although he'd probably prefer the title 'hacker' – called Richard Stallman (Figure 4). According to the story, whilst working in an artificial intelligence (AI) laboratory at MIT in 1979, Stallman wanted to alter some printer software on the lab's Xerox printer. The lab had the binary (machine) code required to run the printer, but not the source code, so it wasn't possible for them to make alterations to the software. When the source code for the printer software was requested in order to make the alteration, the request was refused by Xerox on the grounds that the code was copyright protected. Stallman was incensed. He saw this as an infringement of his personal liberty. Being a hacker, he was well aware of the implications of being refused access to source code; he felt that people should have the right to alter their software in the same way that they have the right to decorate their homes.

Recall that MIT stands for Massachusetts Institute of Technology.

Figure 4   Richard Stallman

Salon was one of the first internet magazines.

About two years later, a few of Stallman's colleagues left the AI lab to set up a company called Symbolics, selling AI workstations. Stallman was horrified by their acceptance and exploitation of intellectual property and copyright laws. Looking back on this time, a 1998 *Salon* article called 'The saint of free software' (the title of which gives an impression of the software developer community's esteem for Richard Stallman) quotes Stallman as saying:

> When I saw the prospect of living the way the rest of the world was living [...] I decided no way, that's disgusting, I'd be ashamed of myself. If I contributed to the upkeep of that other

proprietary software way of life, I'd feel I was making the world ugly for pay.

Richard Stallman, quoted in Leonard, 1998

Free for all

In 1983, Stallman stopped working for MIT and announced the GNU project. He wrote a manifesto in which he described the project. It opened with the following text:

What's GNU? Gnu's Not Unix!

GNU, which stands for Gnu's Not Unix, is the name for the complete Unix-compatible software system which I am writing so that I can give it away free to everyone who can use it. Several other volunteers are helping me. Contributions of time, money, programs and equipment are greatly needed.

Stallman, 1985

Unix was an operating system owned by *American Telephone and Telegraph (AT&T)* that was very popular at the time. It has quite a complex history but was essentially closed source.

Put simply, the GNU project's goal was to produce free software. However, when talking in the context of open source, I have to be careful about what I mean when I say 'free'. Here I quote from the GNU website:

As you might guess, the term *closed source* (or *proprietary*) refers to products where the source code is not made available.

"Free software" is a matter of liberty, not price. To understand the concept, you should think of "free" as in "free speech", not as in "free beer".

Free software is a matter of the users' freedom to run, copy, distribute, study, change and improve the software. More precisely, it means that the program's users have the four essential freedoms:

- The freedom to run the program, for any purpose (freedom 0).
- The freedom to study how the program works, and change it to make it do what you wish (freedom 1). [...]
- The freedom to redistribute copies so you can help your neighbor (freedom 2).
- The freedom to distribute copies of your modified versions to others (freedom 3). By doing this you can give the whole community a chance to benefit from your changes. [...]

A program is free software if users have all of these freedoms. Thus, you should be free to redistribute copies, either with or without modifications, either gratis or charging a fee for distribution, to anyone anywhere. Being free to do these things means (among other things) that you do not have to ask or pay for permission to do so.

You should also have the freedom to make modifications and use them privately in your own work or play, without even mentioning that they exist. If you do publish your changes, you should not be required to notify anyone in particular, or in any particular way.

Free Software Foundation, 2010

Activity 12 (self-assessment)

Looking at the bulleted list of the four freedoms above, which would require access to the source code?

Figure 5 Copyleft symbol

Stallman used the term *copyleft* (as opposed to copyright) to describe the form of protection required to meet the conditions stated above. In order to prevent someone else from copying the code and asserting their own copyright, there had to be some protection; hence the need for copyleft. The symbol for copyright but with the letter c reversed is often used to indicate a copyleft product (Figure 5).

Despite its name, copyleft is a licence – or, to be more precise, a type of licence. There are many different varieties of copyleft licence; Box 1 describes a few of them.

Box 1 Licence agreements in open source

There are various copyleft licence agreements that you will come across when working with open source materials, and quite a few different names to describe them. For example, GNU was released under what is called a *general public licence (GPL)*.

It's worth making the point that in addition to giving users the four freedoms, the GPL makes it clear that derivative works have to provide the same freedoms; this effectively passes on the GPL to any work that contains, or is based on, GPL-protected material.

You will also see the term *Creative Commons licence* used in connection with things that are not software, but that are licensed in a similar way to open source software.

GNU

Unix was considered to be a very well-designed operating system, and it was used very widely so compatibility was highly desirable.

As already mentioned, at the centre of Stallman's GNU project was to be an operating system called GNU that would be compatible with Unix. Writing an operating system is a massive undertaking; Bruce Perens (one of Stallman's former colleagues) has compared it to 'building a jet plane from scratch in his garage'. Operating systems of the time typically consisted of 10 000 lines of code; today, that could be 20 million!

Stallman, along with other developers, worked tirelessly to produce GNU for the next nine years. By 1992 all the major components of the system were complete except for the kernel. The *kernel* is the heart of an operating system; it sits between the computer's hardware (CPU, memory and devices) and its applications (see Figure 6). According to Stallman's plan, something called the GNU Hurd was to be the GNU kernel.

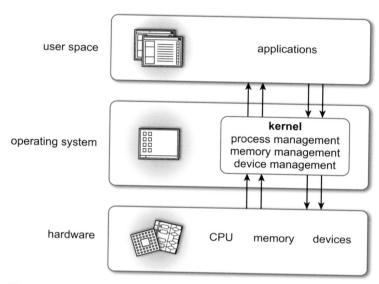

Figure 6   The role of the kernel in a computer

During this time, Stallman had often slept in his office and rarely left his computer. His hands eventually hurt so much from using the keyboard that he was forced to dictate the code. He employed MIT undergraduates to type, but they found the work tedious and didn't stay long. Eventually he was forced to stop. This might have been the end of the matter, if not for another very determined young man.

2.2   A hobbyist

A Finnish undergraduate student at the University of Helsinki called Linus Torvalds found the source code for an operating system called MINIX in a popular textbook (*Operating Systems: Design and Implementation* by Andrew S. Tanenbaum). MINIX first appeared in 1987 as a cut-down Unix-like operating system for academic use, which could be run on (amongst other machines) the relatively cheap IBM-compatible PCs. MINIX had a large and very active news group (MINIX Usenet), and on 25 August 1991 Linus Torvalds sent the following message to it.

From: torvalds@klaava.Helsinki.FI (Linus Benedict Torvalds)
Newsgroups: comp.os.minix
Subject: What would you like to see most in minix?
Summary: small poll for my new operating system

Message-ID: <1991Aug25.205708.9541@klaava.Helsinki.FI>
Date: 25 Aug 91 20:57:08 GMT
Organization: University of Helsinki

Hello everybody out there using minix –

I'm doing a (free) operating system (just a hobby, won't be big and professional like gnu) for 386(486) AT clones. This has been brewing since april, and is starting to get ready. I'd like any feedback on things people like/dislike in minix, as my OS resembles it somewhat (same physical layout of the file-system (due to practical reasons) among other things).

I've currently ported bash(1.08) and gcc(1.40), and things seem to work. This implies that I'll get something practical within a few months, and I'd like to know what features most people would want. Any suggestions are welcome, but I won't promise I'll implement them :-)

Linus (torvalds@kruuna.helsinki.fi)

PS. Yes – it's free of any minix code, and it has a multi-threaded fs. It is NOT portable (uses 386 task switching etc), and it probably never will support anything other than AT-harddisks, as that's all I have :-(.

Torvalds, 1991a

There are some technical references here that need not bother you too much (for instance, both bash(1.08) and gcc(1.40) are part of GNU), but the gist is clear: Torvalds wants to develop an operating system that will run on an IBM PC-compatible computer (hence the reference to 386 and 486, which were the processors used by PC-compatible machines at the time) and he's seeking feedback from the MINIX news group.

The following month, Torvalds released Linux version 0.0.1 and put it on the internet. Along with version 0.0.2 came this famous message in the MINIX news group:

From: torvalds@klaava.Helsinki.FI (Linus Benedict Torvalds)
Newsgroups: comp.os.minix
Subject: Free minix-like kernel sources for 386-AT
Message-ID: <1991Oct5.054106.4647@klaava.Helsinki.FI>
Date: 5 Oct 91 05:41:06 GMT
Organization: University of Helsinki

Do you pine for the nice days of minix-1.1, when men were men and wrote their own device drivers? Are you without a nice project and just dying to cut your teeth on a OS you can try to modify for your needs? Are you finding it frustrating when everything works on minix? No more all-nighters to get a nifty program working? Then this post might be just for you :-)

As I mentioned a month(?) ago, I'm working on a free version of a minix-lookalike for AT-386 computers. It has finally reached the stage where it's even usable (though may not be depending on what you want), and I am willing to put out the sources for wider distribution. It is just version 0.02 (+1 (very small) patch already), but I've successfully run bash/gcc/gnu-make/gnu-sed/compress etc under it.

Sources for this pet project of mine can be found at nic.funet.fi (128.214.6.100) in the directory /pub/OS/Linux. The directory also contains some README-file and a couple of binaries to work under linux (bash, update and gcc, what more can you ask for :-). Full kernel source is provided, as no minix code has been used. Library sources are only partially free, so that cannot be distributed currently. The system is able to compile "as-is" and has been known to work. Heh. Sources to the binaries (bash and gcc) can be found at the same place in /pub/gnu.

Torvalds, 1991b

The significant points here are that Torvalds is making it clear that he is releasing the source code and that it no longer depends on MINIX.

From this stage onwards, things started to move quite rapidly. Within weeks, hundreds of people were offering contributions; this became thousands, and eventually hundreds of thousands.

GNU-Linux

So, Linux took on the role of the kernel for the GNU project and an operating system was born. Hence the correct way to refer to Linux is as GNU-Linux. One of the reasons that Linux has been so successful as a server operating system is that it is extremely reliable. Stability is critical to a server, since many users would be inconvenienced by crashes and levels of activity can be very high, making failures much more likely. Many Linux servers run for years without the need for rebooting.

In his famous book *The Cathedral & the Bazaar* (1999), Eric Raymond writes:

> Given enough eyeballs, all bugs are shallow.

What he means is that with a large enough developer community, it is always possible to identify and remove software bugs quickly. This is key to the success of Linux because it leads to reliability. The user and developer communities are continually testing and repairing defects, and they do it in very large numbers. There are hundreds of thousands of developers and many more users who take the time to report bugs. It's also worth emphasising that Linux doesn't just appear in PCs and servers; it is in a huge range of popular devices including wristwatches, ebook readers, digital TV receivers, mobile phones, cameras, PDAs and satellite navigation systems (to name but a few).

Raymond's book contrasts traditional approaches to software development, where a restricted team of programmers develop and maintain a piece of software (the cathedral), with the open source approach where, potentially, anyone can contribute (the bazaar).

Activity 13 (self-assessment)

Based on what you've learned so far, what do you think are the three key reasons for the success of GNU-Linux?

The author of MINIX, Andrew Tanenbaum, never forgave Linus Torvalds for subverting the MINIX news group and never really agreed with his approach to operating system design. At the root of the dispute was a serious issue over the architecture of the Linux operating system, which was fundamentally different from that of MINIX. In 1992 Tanenbaum wrote:

> I still maintain the point that designing a monolithic kernel in 1991 is a fundamental error. Be thankful you are not my student. You would not get a high grade for such a design :-)

Many messages were exchanged publicly between Tanenbaum and Torvalds in what appeared at the time to be quite a bitter disagreement. At one point Tanenbaum even referred to Linux as 'obsolete', which given its current success seems a little short-sighted. What was taking place seems to have been a *paradigm shift* in software development. As with all paradigm shifts, many of the people immersed in the existing community failed to see its value or move with the change.

Recall that you met the term 'paradigm shift' in Part 2 of this block.

As you've already read, GNU-Linux remains a very popular operating system with hundreds of thousands of contributors and millions of users. The key people involved in its creation, Richard Stallman and Linus Torvalds, were both motivated by a love of software. Both wanted to ensure free access to source code so that they could have the personal freedom to continue to indulge that love. Particularly in the case of Stallman, there was also a political dimension to that motivation which, in part, rejected the notion of using software to generate personal wealth through *intellectual property rights (IPR)* protection.

 ## Activity 14 (exploratory)

In the resources page associated with this part on the TU100 website, you'll find a five-minute video in which Stephen Fry compares free software to the freedom to alter your plumbing. Watch this video now. Is Fry's view consistent with the view that open source software is 'free' as in 'free speech' rather than as in 'free beer'?

Comment

Yes. It's the freedom to do what you want with it, rather than acquiring it at no cost, that he is referring to.

Incidentally this video was, of course, released under a Creative Commons licence very similar to those used by the open source community. I will talk a little more about Creative Commons licences later in the part.

2.3 Other open source projects

Linux is one of the most successful open source initiatives, but it is far from being the only one. For instance, you might at some time have used a browser called Firefox, or used Open Office (the open source equivalent to Microsoft Office). In this section I will look at Firefox and some other open source projects.

Firefox

The history of Firefox is very different from that of Linux. Firefox is a product of the Mozilla Foundation, which was established in 2003 as a 'not-for-profit corporation dedicated to public benefit'. However, it has its roots in a closed source browser called Netscape Navigator.

It may seem odd from today's perspective, but in the mid-1990s web browsers were just beginning to become items of commercial importance and interest. At this time, Netscape Navigator was the most popular choice of browser. However, during the late 1990s Microsoft's Internet Explorer emerged and eventually dominated the market (though only after a legal manoeuvre that claimed it was not possible to make Microsoft's then current operating system, Windows 98, work without IE being embedded).

In 1998, Netscape created the Mozilla Organization and released most of the source code for its browser under an open source licence. In 2003 Mozilla established the Mozilla Foundation, followed in 2005 by a wholly owned subsidiary company – the Mozilla Corporation – which looks after Firefox.

In much the same way as Linux, Firefox is maintained by a large community of developers with a very clear and quite hierarchical organisational structure that supports its development. However, the obvious difference between the histories of GNU-Linux and Firefox is that GNU-Linux started as an open source product, whereas Firefox grew out of Netscape Navigator (which was closed source).

Firefox currently accounts for between 19% and 33% of the recorded usage share of web browsers, depending on where you look for figures. Box 2 discusses some of the problems that are inherent in trying to measure the usage share of different browsers.

At the time of writing, Microsoft is offering consumers the option to choose an alternative browser and this is having some impact on the usage share.

Box 2 Beware the numbers

When you visit a website, your browser identifies itself to the web server by sending a string or series of characters. Information about the number of times a particular browser is used to visit each site is collected by web services such as Net Applications and StatCounter. The 'recorded usage share' is the number of requests for pages made by particular types of browser. The figures for recorded usage share vary, partly because it is a measure of which browsers are requesting information and not of how many users are using a particular browser.

Figures such as the usage share for Firefox are notoriously inaccurate. In this case they are a measure of how many requests came from which browsers over a large number of servers. The problem is that not all browsers work in the same way: some will request more information than others, not all users configure their browsers to operate in the same way, and the browsing habits of users vary.

So why should the browsing habits of users matter in such a survey? The answer is that they wouldn't if the users' habits were uniformly distributed across the different types of browser. But Internet Explorer is given freely with Windows, so people who take the trouble to change to another browser such as Firefox have to make an effort to do so. This probably means that they are more skilled and experienced, and so it is likely that they spend more time using the Web. This would tend to exaggerate the number of Firefox users.

Of course, I am only using this as an example and there are many other factors that can skew the figures. The message is simple – you should always treat such figures with scepticism.

Activity 15 (self-assessment)

(a) What is meant by the phrase 'recorded usage share'?

(b) Why might the figure for recorded usage share not be an accurate representation of the market share for a particular browser?

The important point is that at the time of writing (2010), Firefox is the second most popular browser after Internet Explorer.

Apache

The Apache HTTP Server project is another open source project whose product is very widely used. The chances are that you have, unknowingly, used this software nearly every time you have browsed the Web.

According to Netcraft, currently (in 2010) something like half of the world's web servers use Apache HTTP Server (often referred to simply as Apache). This is consistent with other sources and is probably a quite accurate figure.

Apache HTTP Server is the software that distributes objects such as web pages when you request them by clicking on a link or typing a URL into a browser. The server software upon which Apache HTTP Server was based was developed from a piece of software called the http daemon (httpd) at the National Center for Supercomputing Applications (NCSA) based at the University of Illinois. When the original author of httpd, Rob McCool, left the NCSA in 1994 the software was left unsupported but in widespread use. Apache claims that by February 1995 it was the most popular server software available, powering something like 95% of all web servers.

The NCSA has a long history of providing useful tools free to the computing community.

To begin with httpd existed as public domain software (Box 3). Yet inevitably, as time went by various things needed fixing in httpd and, although bugs were being fixed, nobody was coordinating the activity. In 1995 a group of *webmasters* in California linked up to provide *patches* and bug fixes, and formed the foundation of what became the Apache group. The Apache group then released the software under an open source licence, and as with Linux and Firefox the list of contributors grew. Today Apache still dominates the server software market and currently lists over 80 other software projects.

> ## Box 3 Public domain software
>
> Public domain software is software that has not been copylefted. In other words, although it is freely distributed by the author, a software company could compile the code into a binary executable and sell it on without passing on the source code.
>
> Put simply, public domain software is more vulnerable to proprietary exploitation than copylefted software.

Ubiquitous computing and open source

In 2008, the mobile phone company Nokia helped to establish the non-profit Symbian Foundation. This foundation draws its members from companies with a wide range of interests in mobile phones, including Nokia, AT&T, LG, Motorola, NTT Docomo, Samsung, Sony Ericsson, STMicroelectronics, Texas Instruments and Vodafone. The foundation was formed to oversee the development of the Symbian operating system and also to facilitate its transition to open source, which occurred in

February 2010. Lee Williams, head of the Symbian Foundation, was quoted by the BBC as saying:

> When we chatted to companies who develop third party applications, we found people would spend up to nine months just trying to navigate the intellectual property [...] That was really hindering the rate of progress.

Fildes, 2010

So, one of the reasons for Symbian's move to open source was to make the products of Nokia and other mobile phone companies more competitive by freeing up the development of applications that could run on them.

Two points to note in the Symbian story are as follows.

- The operating system went from being closed source to open source. Projects that do this are not uncommon.

- It was hoped that sales of phones would be increased by allowing more innovation.

SourceForge

As a contrast to Linux, Firefox and Apache, I want to close this section by briefly describing SourceForge. SourceForge is owned and operated by Geeknet Inc., a publicly traded company based in the USA. It was launched in late 1999, at a time when the *dotcom boom* was at its height and people were investing in anything that related to exploiting the internet with very little idea as to how (or even if) they'd see a return on their investment. The thinking behind SourceForge was similar to that of selling pans to gold miners during the gold rush.

Activity 16 (exploratory)

What do you understand by the analogy of selling pans to gold miners?

Comment

Selling essential equipment is a more certain source of income than prospecting for gold. Shops would sell miners everything they needed in order to go prospecting. Similarly, SourceForge provides everything one would need in order to create an open source project.

So what does it do? SourceForge is a site devoted to supporting open source software projects. It provides space to host the development, software to support developers, facilities to help distribute the software and, vitally, access to a community of about two million users, many of whom are software developers. In February 2009 it claimed to have over 230 000 registered software projects.

With this level of activity, it's not surprising that many significant pieces of software have emerged from SourceForge over the last 10 years, such as eMule (a peer-to-peer document-sharing application) and VLC media player (a multimedia player for most video and audio formats). SourceForge is not alone in offering an environment for the development of open source software but, in 2010, it is the most active.

2.4   Conclusion

Firefox and Linux are among the most high-profile open source projects, but they are just two of many. The total number of open source software projects currently in existence is in the hundreds of thousands. Many of these projects are very successful without having a particularly high public profile.

Eventually I want to discuss how many of these projects manage to generate an income, but before I do that I'd like to explore how open source projects function, who contributes to them and what their motives are. Along the way I want to introduce you to some tools that will be helpful when thinking about complex organisations.

This session should have helped you with the following learning outcomes.

- Explain the purpose of licensing.
- Name and give a brief history of some important open source projects.

3 The structure of open source projects

As you've already seen, the open source movement works in a very different way from a mainstream software business such as Microsoft or Electronic Arts (which produces computer games). From the discussion so far, you might wonder how it is possible for open source projects to generate income or to function commercially – and yet they do.

In this session I want to think more generally about how open source initiatives can function sustainably. In order to do this, I'm going to construct a general *model* of an open source production system; but first, I want to draw your attention to some aspects of *systems* and of *models*.

3.1 Thinking in terms of models and systems

Models

Models are central to the ways in which we learn and think.

Activity 17 (exploratory)

Think for a moment about what you understand by the term 'model'. Jot down some examples of different kinds of model.

Comment

The word 'model' is in everyday use, yet it has lots of different meanings. It can refer, for example, to a child's wooden model of a farm with all its animals, a scale replica of a Spitfire, an experimental model such as a number of water tanks connected by plastic pipes, or many other types of physical construction. Alternatively, a model can be a set of mathematical equations used to predict the spread of an epidemic, a diagram of a proposed new organisational structure for a company, a computer model showing the interior layout of a building, or the spreadsheet model of my home finances.

Do the different uses of the term 'model' listed in the previous activity have anything in common? If so, what is it? What is a model, anyway?

My definition of a model is as follows:

> A simplified representation of something, constructed for a specific purpose.

There are two points to note about this definition: the first is that a model is a *simplified* representation of something that is more (usually much more) complex, while the second is that a model is constructed for a particular *purpose*. The latter point means that different purposes may require different models. For example, a model Spitfire designed to hang in a child's bedroom would be constructed rather differently from a radio-controlled model Spitfire that was designed to fly. Likewise, a spreadsheet model recording the work of staff in a factory for the purpose of paying them correctly would differ from a diagrammatic model showing the different types of work undertaken by different staff groups for the purpose of evaluating health and safety risks. In both cases the same thing (Spitfire or work of staff) is being modelled in different ways, using models that are appropriate to their purpose.

Activity 18 (self-assessment)

Make a list of the sorts of model you have encountered so far in this section.

Since a model is a simplified representation of a more complex reality, a crucial question about any model is how good it is – that is, how well it represents reality. One cannot answer this question, however, without knowing the purpose for which the model was designed. For example, a very crude sketch map of Britain will be perfectly adequate for the purpose of showing a tourist where Scotland is in relation to Wales, but it will be of no use whatsoever for deciding whether Birdcage Walk is north or south of Buckingham Palace. This is obviously a silly example, but I am sure you get the point.

You have already seen that there are various sorts of model. There are physical models that architects make to demonstrate a design to a client. There are analogue models constructed to show the workings of a complex or mysterious system in terms of more familiar objects; thus scientists sometimes model the molecules in a gas as sets of animated billiard balls, while engineers talk about the 'flow' of current around a circuit or about electrical charge 'accumulating' in a capacitor. And there are mathematical models, in which some actual system is represented by a set of equations whose solution yields behaviour (hopefully) similar to that observed in real-life systems.

Yet models are not just things that engineers and scientists use. Models are essentially what we all think with. We carry in our heads representations of real people, situations and events that are to some extent simplified: they are models of the people, situations or events. What's more, the process of learning involves the acquisition of new models and/or the modification of existing ones.

In the case of the open source system I want to model, my purpose is to gain a better insight into how open source projects function. In this case my model will take the form of a diagram, which I will construct shortly. Diagramming, that is the *process* of drawing a diagram, provides a good way of externalising (representing) mental models so that I can think about them more effectively and discuss them with others.

Before I do that, however, I want to talk a little about systems. I said at the beginning of this session that I wanted to construct a general *model* of an open source production *system*. Now I want to explain what I mean by a system.

Systems

Throughout this text the term 'system' keeps cropping up, often in the phrase *operating system* but also occasionally on its own. So what do I mean when I say system?

The word system is in regular everyday use. People talk, for example, about 'the social security system' and 'telecommunication systems'. Gamblers boast about 'having a system' for winning at roulette. Parents talk about the 'childcare system'. But the trouble with everyday speech is that it is often imprecise: people mean different things by the same word. When a gambler speaks of having an infallible system for winning, for example, he or she is using the term in a different sense from an engineer who works on the telephone system. Since the concept of 'system' is central to so much technological and scientific thinking, we can't afford the potential confusion that this might cause. We need an agreed definition of system.

Activity 19 (exploratory)

What do you understand by the term 'system'? Before proceeding, make an attempt at a definition by writing a sentence that begins 'A system is ...'.

Comment

My sentence is as follows: 'A system is a group of components that are connected in some way and that perform some kind of function.' Your sentence will be different, but I hope you have included the main ideas of *components*, *connectedness* and *function*.

At this point I want to introduce a formal definition of a system. The definition that I use has four parts:

1   A system is an assembly of components connected together in an organised way.

2   The components are affected by being in the system and are changed if they leave it.

3   The assembly of components does something.

4   The assembly has been identified by a human as being of interest.

These all seem straightforward enough, but they each have important implications. Let's examine them in turn.

1   A system is an assembly of components connected together in an organised way

The stress here is on the word 'organised'. This means, for example, that the components of a clock piled together in a heap on a table awaiting assembly do not constitute a system. After assembly, however, they do make up a system because their interconnections have been organised.

2   The components are affected by being in the system and are changed if they leave it

As an example of this, think of the physiological system that is your body. Its components are organs such as your heart, liver, kidneys and lungs. Clearly they are changed if they are removed from the system: they decay, they become inert and lifeless.

So far, so good. But actually this part of the definition has very far-reaching implications. For if the components are different in some way when they're in the system from when they're not, then the system as a whole must have properties that cannot be deduced or predicted from an inspection of its components taken in isolation. One common way of putting this is to say that 'the whole (i.e. the system) is greater than the sum of its parts'.

Let's think about this for a moment, using as an example the problem of picking a national rugby team. In theory, the correct way to do this would be to select the best individual players – the best scrum half, the best full back and so on – in the country and bring them together. The trouble with this is that somehow they don't seem to mesh well as a team. Their joint performance is not as good as you would expect, given the abilities of the individual players; the system seems to have some special property that can be observed in the disappointing performance of the side. Observation of this effect has prompted some people to speculate on whether it might be better (if it were possible) to simply pick the entire current Bath (or whatever) side and let that team represent the country instead! For although the players might not be as good individually as their international counterparts, their overall performance as a team might be much better.

What does this example show? Firstly, I think it illustrates my claim that the whole system might have certain properties that are different from what you might expect based on the individual components. Secondly, the example shows that 'the whole is greater than the sum of its parts' is not a good way of describing the effect. In the case of the team, the performance of the whole side is less than the sum of its individual members – and besides, the word 'sum' isn't a particularly good way of describing the players' interaction.

For reasons like these, a word has been invented to describe the special properties that 'wholes' or systems seem to have. This word is *synergy*. The adjective based on it is 'synergistic'; thus we could refer to a team's disappointing performance as a synergistic effect or property of the system.

Synergy means that we have to be very careful in analysing a system. In particular, it means that it is not sufficient to analyse the system's various components in isolation from one another: we must also consider what happens when they are linked together in an organised way. This is effectively summarised in Figure 7, in which the parts bear very little relation to their 'sum'.

Figure 7   Synergy

This isn't just an abstract idea: it has real practical implications. Take, for example, the performance of your internet connection. You might find that your connection is far too slow and attribute this to the quality of your Wi-Fi system. Given that high-performance Wi-Fi systems are relatively cheap, an obvious solution seems to be to install such a system in your home. Surely that would improve the connection speed considerably? Actually, it might not – and the reason again is something to do with the nature of the network system. The connection speed depends on a host of different components working as a system; changing one in isolation will improve the situation only if the other components (your computer, your ISP and your phone line) are delivering appropriate bandwidth.

3   The assembly of components does something

What this means is that the things called systems are not, in general, inactive. They are dynamic in some way: processes of one sort or another go on within them. Thus under this part of the definition we would not call a chessboard a system, though it might be a component of a system that includes players and pieces.

Note, however, that a system might *appear* to be doing nothing much. A person in a coma, for example, will appear pretty lifeless; yet all kinds of processes (temperature regulation, metabolism, breathing, blood circulation, etc.) will be going on within the body.

4   The assembly has been identified by a human as being of interest
This is important because it brings out the fact that a system is essentially a private, personal idea. A system can be (and often is) simply a personal ordering of reality, the result of seeing some degree of orderly interconnectedness in some part of the world. Thus a system – any system – can be many different kinds of system simultaneously, depending on who is studying it and why. For instance, the telecommunication system is a communication system for its users, a technical system and an employment system for BT engineers, and so on.

In principle this concept of 'system' is quite simple, but I hope you can begin to see why it has important implications. I hope, too, that you will use the word with some care. For example, you should not use the term to describe something in which the components are not linked in an organised way. And you should learn to be suspicious of any analysis of the components of a technological system that concentrates only on their individual properties without considering the question of how they might interact with one another.

Activity 20 (self-assessment)

Fill in the blanks using the words below. Try to do this without referring back to the definitions given in the main text.

affected   assembly   enter   human   interact   purpose   system

There are four elements in the definition of a _____:

1   it should consist of an _____ of components that _____

2   the components are _____ if they are removed from or _____ the assembly

3   the assembly should have a _____

4   the assembly should have been identified as being of interest to a _____.

3.2   Modelling an open source system

Let's try to look at the open source development of Linux as a system of interconnected components or entities. I need to decide what these entities might be, and then look at the different types of relationship (or connection) between them. By doing this I'll gradually build a description of an open source production system.

In working through the definition of a system from the previous section, I'm not going to take the four elements in order. I think it makes more sense to work with the list in reverse order, although in practice you will find that if you follow the list in either order you will iterate several times before arriving at a description.

So starting with item 4, this assembly is undoubtedly of human interest: books and magazines abound that talk about open source and Linux. In fact, I should take care to remember that some of what I say will be coloured by my own worldview. This is a necessary part of my describing open source production of Linux as a system.

Looking at item 3, the assembly clearly has a purpose, but Linux – rather like the telecommunications example above – is many things to many people. Thus programmers might consider it as a way of deriving income, enjoying a hobby and/or building a reputation, businesses as a product, end users as a free operating system and system administrators as a stable platform for software. Here I want to look at the entities that support the development of Linux and help to sustain it as a product. So the purpose of the system I'll describe is to produce and sustain the GNU-Linux project.

So what are the entities that make up my system? There could be many things and many people involved. Here I want to focus on the roles of individuals who contribute in some way to the product. Remember that for this assembly to be a system, these individuals must interact (item 1) and should affect the assembly if they enter or leave it (item 2).

Activity 21 (exploratory)

Make a list of roles that people may take in creating, supplying and using Linux.

Comment

Roles include software developer, vendor, supplier, user and organiser.

Key roles

Let's start at the heart of the project. Each new development of the operating system requires approval, and this is the primary responsibility of Linus Torvalds. Yes, after 20 years Torvalds still remains the key decision-making figure in the development process.

As you know, there are also thousands of software developers who contribute to the project, so clearly the role of software developer is key too. These software developers are part of a large online community who offer their collective skills to sustain the project. I will explore some of the motives behind this in the next subsection.

I've shown the relationship between Torvalds and the developers in Figure 8. You will see that I've used the symbol of a gate to represent the approval process. The arrows in the diagram indicate a flow; in this case, you can regard the flow as being the product moving through the development process. As I said earlier, the model I am constructing of this system is in the form of a diagram. Usually diagrams are regarded as devices for effective communication ('a picture speaks a thousand words') and that is certainly the case here; however, it's not the only reason for using a diagram. The process of drawing a diagram can be an extremely valuable thinking tool for better understanding a complex situation.

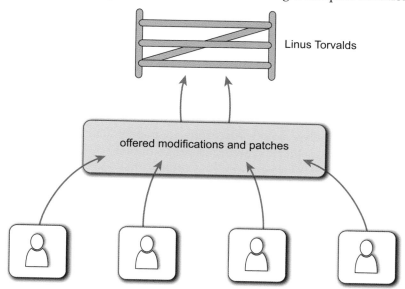

Figure 8   **Developers offer modifications and patches that are worked upon, then passed forward for inclusion as a part of Linux**

So, starting at the bottom of Figure 8, we have software developers offering modifications for Linux. These modifications cover a whole range of possibilities, but they need not concern us here; all that matters is that they are offerings in the form of code. Once offered, the modifications are tested and maybe improved by other developers, and then eventually approved by Linus Torvalds for distribution. In this sense you can think of Torvalds as an organiser.

This is already a gross simplification, since there will be many different aspects to the modifications and individual groups will be working on particular developments. But it does capture the basic process.

Developers

So who are the developers? In the case of Linux, the answer to this is that they are a very large number of skilled programmers with a wide range of motivations. The significant feature of the Linux development process is that employers are not an explicit part of it. Some of the contributors are not even paid to write software for Linux; they do it for other reasons. Given that the final product is so dependent on them, it is worth stopping to examine their motives, at the root of which are *values* (Box 4).

CODE stands for Collaboration and Ownership in the Digital Economy.

Box 4 Motivations

Throughout the story of open source initiatives I will keep returning to values. Many of the people who started the movement did so because of personally held values relating to freedom, like Richard Stallman. You have seen this already when you looked at the history of open source, but it is worth bearing in mind throughout your reading of this section.

Speaking at the CODE conference in Cambridge in 2001, Bruce Perens – a particularly famous open source contributor – described his motivations as being that he loved to write computer code and that it was 'really cool' that his software was floating around in space (it was used on board the space shuttle). This is fairly typical of the first impression one gets of open source contributors; they're people who do it because they love it. Also, they are people who gain the respect of their peers (in this case other programmers) by being seen to do it. There exists a list of Linux contributors that you can find and view online, and it is understood by the Linux community that being seen as a contributor is helpful in acquiring status and employment in the world of software developers. You will see some evidence of this when I discuss business models for Linux and talk about consultancy. Some of these people may well be 'moonlighting' – that is, contributing at the same time as working for companies that either don't realise or possibly don't mind.

Traditionally, it seems, very few contributors received payment as a *direct* consequence of their contributions, although evidence that this was really the case is not easy to find. I say 'traditionally' because there has been a gradual shift in emphasis and now many companies are happy to *pay* their employees to contribute! Certainly this isn't done out of altruism; companies such as IBM and Intel see real value in this sort of activity. Many of these companies use Linux as an operating system on hardware products that they sell. Andrew Morton was lead maintainer for the *Linux production kernel* in 2004 and he observed that of the 38 000 most recent patches, 97% were made by about 100 developers and these were employees paid by companies to work on Linux (Deek and McHugh, 2007, p. 95).

You probably won't be surprised to learn that most personal computers use Microsoft Windows operating systems (I estimate about 90% in 2010, based on several sources). However, when we look at other types of computer the distribution is very different, with Linux being totally dominant for supercomputers and holding a significant market share for embedded systems, servers and routers. If products such as servers and routers are going to depend on open source operating systems then these systems need to be reliable, and that means there has to be support. This is why large companies such

It's worth recalling at this stage that projects such as Firefox and Apache were once proprietary and have since become open source.

as IBM are willing to pay staff to contribute to a product from which they derive no *direct* profit.

This goes some way towards explaining what appears to be a free contribution from the commercial world, but there is also another dimension: Linux, like any other open source product, has end users. These could include IBM using Linux as an operating system for a server, a company choosing to sell personal computers that run Linux, or an individual deciding to use Linux as an operating system. The business opportunities involved in the first two of these are fairly obvious: the companies generate revenue from the sale of the hardware and product support. But there are also some interesting possibilities in the case of an individual choosing to use Linux on a personal computer.

Linux has traditionally been seen as a rather complex operating system that requires specialist knowledge to use. In the late 1990s, a company called Red Hat™ emerged that provided specialist support and training for Linux users who paid a subscription. The company, which when it went public in 1999 showed the eighth biggest first-day gain in share value in the history of Wall Street, became hugely successful. This demonstrates another of the ways in which open source initiatives can generate money, this time by adding value to the product. Again, Red Hat employees also contribute to the development of Linux; in fact, at the time of writing, the company remains one of the biggest contributors. Companies such as Canonical, which sponsors Ubuntu, have a similar business model.

Returning to my original model, I need to add a section to show how the output is used and the ways in which organisations add value to generate an income (Figure 9). I have also added dashed arrows connecting the companies to employees. The employees are contributing based on their knowledge of the shortcomings and needs that the company identifies.

I also need to include the motivational aspect of open source development in my model (Figure 10). This time the blue arrows represent not the flow of the product but either money or esteem. I have labelled the section on the right-hand side as the list of contributors. Physically it is the place where the work of individual contributors is cited. This is equivalent to the end credits for a TV programme.

You can see that at both the developer stage and the delivery stage there are many participants with different perspectives on what the project should be or what it delivers. One of the remarkable things about the Linux project is that it has never split to become several different versions with different groups supporting each. Although there are different versions of Linux, the core is the same for all. This is in a large part due

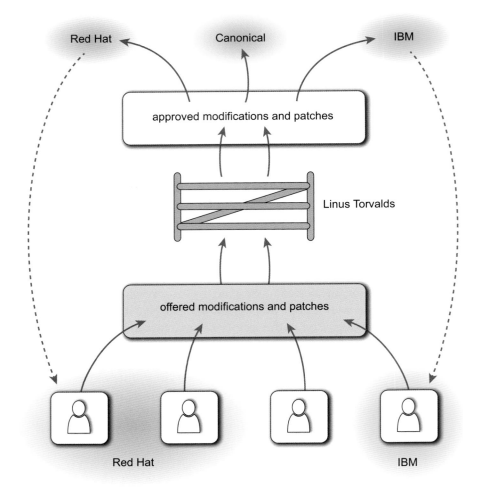

Figure 9   Connection between contributors and companies 'selling' Linux

to the trust that the developer community places in Linus Torvalds, who's responsible for making the key decisions about what to include in each new release. In many ways the developers are acting as a group.

Having completed the model for Linux, I now want to try to generalise it to cover any open source project. I have done this in Figure 11, where you will see that I have simply altered various labels in the diagram in order to make it less specific. Most if not all open source projects have the elements in this diagram in some form. So as you read on through the remaining sessions, you should refer back to this diagram when necessary.

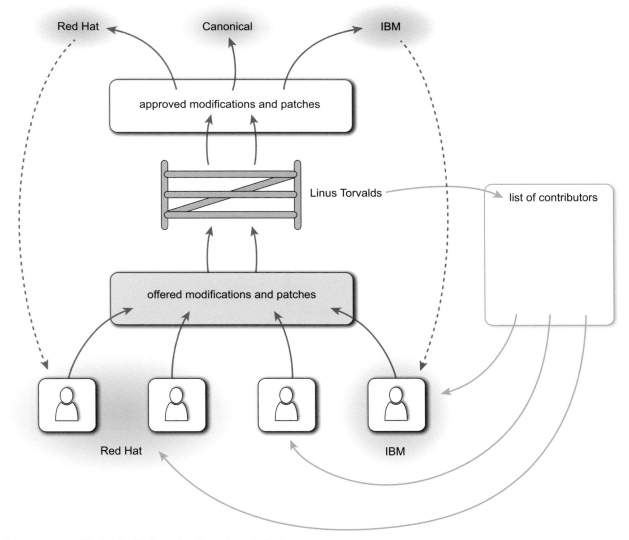

Figure 10   Model including the list of contributors

Activity 22 (self-assessment)

Imagine that the various entities shown in Figure 11 (vendors, quality control, product development and contributors) are engaged in writing an open source encyclopaedia. In a few sentences, describe the role and/or possible nature of each entity.

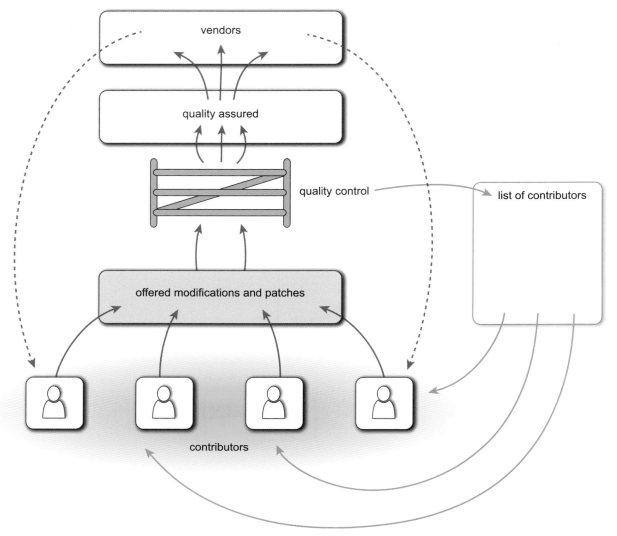

Figure 11   Generalised diagram of the open source development system

3.3 Conclusion

The concepts of models, systems, values and multiple perspectives are all central to systems (or systemic) thinking. In Block 5 the concept of multiple perspectives will be taken up again.

As with all systems, it's the detail of how things are connected together that governs the behaviour of the system. The fact that many of the software developers work for companies that market products that depend on Linux is probably key to its success. In the next session I will explore some of the ways in which companies and individuals derive an income from free and open source software.

This session should have helped you with the following learning outcomes.

- Describe what constitutes a system.
- Develop skills in working with diagrams.
- Describe a simple model for open source development.

4

Open source and the world of business

The question that always arises when discussing open source is 'How does anyone make any money out of it?'. I have talked a little about how software developers are paid to write code, but this doesn't explain how it's possible to make money directly from the product – and yet there are many businesses that do exactly that. It is often said that businesses that make money from open source do so from the 'halo'. The metaphor of a halo here is interesting: it suggests something good radiating from the product, with slightly religious overtones. Nevertheless, it is appropriate, since open source businesses seem to exist around the product rather than contain it. Before I look closely at how they do this I'd like to begin to answer the question, 'If this stuff is free then why doesn't everyone use it?'.

4.1 Vendor lock-in

I opened this part by telling you that I wrote the first draft of this material using Open Office, an open source package equivalent to Microsoft Office. By the second draft I was forced to move to using Microsoft Office. This is because the template that The Open University uses for producing modules is dependent on Microsoft Word to run. You could ask why the OU doesn't simply convert to an equivalent Open Office template, but this is the thin end of a very long wedge – as you will, I hope, see.

The inability to switch between products is often referred to as *vendor lock-in* (Figure 12). It's not just the technical aspects of switching that get in the way; obviously, staff will have invested a lot of time developing experience in using the current applications. Also, Microsoft Office is often seen as a 'safe' decision for an organisation such as The Open University, so there is a mindset that might need to alter too before change can take place.

4.2 Total cost of ownership

As well as the difficulties inherent in switching, it is important to consider the cost of a product – and this is by no means as simple as saying 'X is the best option because it's free'. Costs come in two forms, direct and indirect. A direct cost could be the purchase price of the software itself, although this wouldn't necessarily apply in the case of open source software. Indirect costs could be the time taken to install the software

Figure 12 **Vendor lock-in**

or for staff to learn how to use it. There will be costs in terms of damage to the company's reputation if the software turns out to be unreliable or ineffective. Thus the total cost of owning a piece of software is far more than just the purchase price. In fact, Gartner Group estimated the original purchase price to be less than 10% of the *total cost of ownership*!

Activity 23 (exploratory)

Thinking in terms of software that you own, have you ever encountered either direct or indirect costs beyond the purchase price?

Comment

There's certainly the time it takes to install and learn to use the software. Additionally, it's quite common to incur additional costs for calling a helpline. Usually, but by no means always, if the software is new there will be no charge beyond that of the call – but it still takes time.

For an organisation, it is possible to break the total cost of ownership down into four main categories.

1   *Planning and deployment.* In addition to the purchase cost, this includes aspects such as the need for new hardware, installation and data migration (a company may have to transfer large quantities of data, which could result in downtime for its systems). Then there are the less obvious aspects, such as the cost of making the decision – the time taken to research the possibilities and experiment (it would be very foolish to decide just to buy and install, say, a new piece of database software without testing it first).

2   *Support and learning*. As I have already mentioned, the cost in terms of disruption – such as taking people away from their usual work for training, and the time required to become familiar with the software – can be considerable, especially if you consider that a company may have thousands of staff who all have to learn new skills.

3   *Human resources or people*. These can include consultants, who are often used to advise on which software to buy and how to develop staff to use it.

4   *Ongoing costs*. These can include administration, technical support and professional development.

It's not surprising that companies take a great deal of care when deciding whether to change or upgrade their software!

4.3   Business models

Now we come to the key question: how do people make money from open source? Currently there appear to be five major business models:

1   dual licensing

2   consulting on open source software

3   providing open source software distributions and services

4   hybrid proprietary/open model – vertical development with open source software

5   hybrid proprietary/open model – horizontal arrangements.

I will look at each of these in turn.

Dual licensing

It is quite often the case that we are given free software that is only partially functional. This is common with games software, where after reaching a certain level in the game the user is told 'if you want to go on you'll have to buy the full version'.

Activity 24 (self-assessment)

Look back at the description of the GPL agreement in Section 2.1 (Box 1). Can you see a problem with this approach in an open source context?

MySQL AB is a Swedish company now owned by Sun Microsystems.

However, the problem mentioned in the activity is not a problem if you own the GPL under which the software was released in the first place. This is how MySQL AB, which owns the licence to the database system MySQL, manages to have both an open source version (the popular MySQL) and a proprietary version (SQLPro). The company claims that the proprietary version is more secure and reliable, as well as being supplied with free service support.

There is some risk in this dual strategy, since SQLPro could benefit from the contributions of the open source community as well as MySQL, and this might adversely affect the motivation of contributors. On the other hand, the software undoubtedly benefits from its large developer community and this relationship has worked well over the last 15 years.

The proprietary licence for SQLPro allows commercial distributors to modify the source and to sell it on as a closed source system.

Consulting on open source software

There is a huge range of open source products in existence and many companies depend on them; in some cases, an open source product is the best or only available option. But smaller companies that might depend on various different pieces of open source software would probably struggle with the technical knowhow required to configure and use these products. Companies such as GBDirect, a British consulting firm, offer their expertise across a wide selection of open source products.

Most open source software is developed with a great deal of skill and works well, but the documentation – which is critical to installing and running any software – is often sparse and can be very difficult to follow. This is where consulting companies can make a difference; software often requires modification and adaptation that only a specialist can provide. GBDirect has close links with the open source developer communities and is often able to offer custom modifications for individual users, written by the author of the original software.

Activity 25 (exploratory)

How does GBDirect's business model benefit the developer community?

Comment

It can offer paid work to many of the developers.

Providing open source software distributions and services

Red Hat, which I mentioned in Section 3.2 (Box 4), is a business that has done very well from this model. Unlike GBDirect, Red Hat specialises in a single product, Linux. It sells Linux by packaging it, providing instructions and support in exchange for a subscription. It provides its own distributions of the latest stable versions of Linux, complete with open system components such as *input–output (IO) drivers*, Apache servers and a GUI called X11.

Essentially, businesses that operate using this model rely on having a strong brand name in order to survive. This isn't very far from the business model that Microsoft uses, except that the core product is open source. Given the difficulty that inexperienced users often face in configuring Linux, the Red Hat model makes a lot of sense.

Hybrid proprietary/open models

Horizontal and vertical models of business

If you read a lot of material about economics and management then you would come across references to horizontal and vertical integration. These are two different approaches to management control.

In a vertically integrated structure (Figure 13), all the organisations in the supply chain have the same owner but they all produce different things. For example, in the car industry it might be that every process, from producing the raw materials such as steel, aluminium and paint to the final assembly of vehicles and marketing, is carried out by a chain of companies with a single owner. This is very rare.

Horizontal integration (Figure 14) is much more common. Here many similar products are produced by companies with the same owner. In the case of the car industry, it might be that a single owner manufactures several different brands; for example, Jaguar and Range Rover are both owned by Tata.

In the context of software, the language is used in a similar but subtly different way. In the vertical model, the software is used (and maybe developed) by the company but never emerges as a product, as you will see in the case of Google below. In horizontal development, the software development is shared across different companies (hence horizontal) but, importantly, it is shipped or sold as a part of the individual company's main product. This could be something like a wristwatch or mobile phone running Linux.

Vertical development with open source software

In 2003 Rasmus Lerdorf, creator of the PHP programming language, was asked by ePrairie: 'Is it possible to be a successful, open source software company? If so, what does it take?'. His answer was as follows:

ePrairie was a web-based US technology news column.

> It is possible, I think, but we don't need very many of them. Where the real money is in open source is in the verticals. It's about taking open source software, applying it to a problem and selling the resulting solution. That's where you will find the billion-dollar companies.

Quoted in Schneider, 2003

He may well have had a very good point! Companies such as Google make heavy use of open source software. Recall the answer to the first activity in this part, where I asked when you last used a computer running Linux. The answer in essence was 'possibly when you last did a search using Google, because it uses a lot of Linux servers running Apache'.

trees are cut down
and transported to
the paper mill

the trees are
made into paper

the paper is
printed on and
made into books

the books are
transported to
the shop to sell

Figure 13   **Vertical integration**

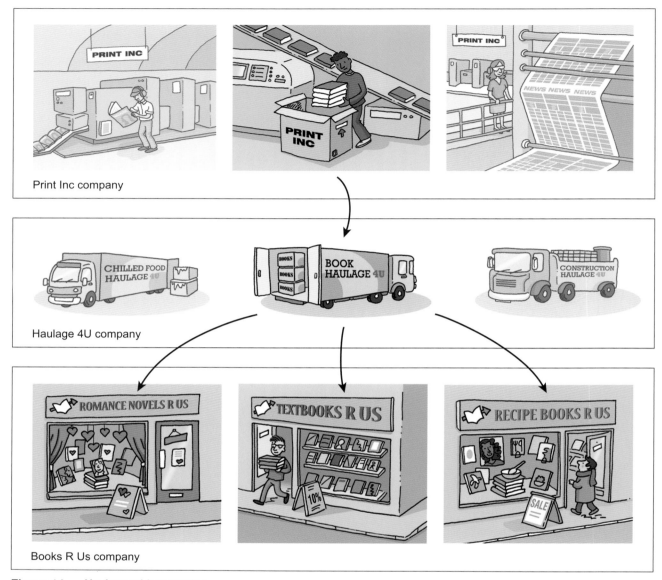

Figure 14   Horizontal integration

This is an example of vertical development. Companies such as Yahoo and Google are not distributing the software; they are using it to provide a service to solve valuable consumer problems. It's also what's driving cloud computing, because companies such as Google are in control of their software. They don't have to worry about a particular vendor no longer supporting their activities or pushing up the prices of licences to tap into their successes.

Horizontal arrangements

Here we have businesses working alongside each other (hence the term horizontal) and the open source community, exploiting and developing open source products to enhance and support their own products. I have already mentioned IBM's use of Linux and Apache to add value to the hardware that it sells, and how this leads to IBM paying programmers to write for Linux. This has to be a carefully managed process, because too much effort and influence on the part of IBM could interfere with the meritocracy so valued by the developer community.

Additionally, some companies use open source software to spread the burdens of cost and risk over a wider community, which includes other companies that need the same product but are not direct competitors.

Activity 26 (self-assessment)

Fill in the blanks using the words below. Try to do this without referring back to the definitions given in the main text.

cloud   developer   open source   proprietary   support

The dual licensing model allows a business to license _____ software that contains open source code.

Consulting companies rely on charging for advising companies on _____ software and helping to customise it.

Companies can package software and add value by including _____ and installation instructions.

Vertical development of hybrid proprietary/open source software enables companies to support activities such as _____ computing.

Companies that collaborate with each other and the _____ community to produce open source software are said to be working horizontally.

4.4   Open source in the wider world

I hope you can already see that open source projects such as GNU-Linux, Apache and Firefox are quite different from conventional business projects. In many ways they simply don't fit with the world of commerce, where companies fiercely defend their products from competitors and the motivations are largely power and personal wealth. However, this does not mean that open source projects are independent of the commercial and political world, and occasionally paths cross with interesting results.

Three such incidents are described below. Two relate to Linux and legal issues, while the third relates to SourceForge and international law. The aspect that is interesting in all three cases is the reaction of the open source community to external threats.

Linux as a trademark

It hasn't all been plain sailing with respect to protecting Linux from the commercial environment in which it exists. In 1996, vendors of Linux began to receive letters from an attorney of William Della Croce, Jr requesting royalties for using the trademark 'Linux'. Della Croce did in fact own the Linux trademark and had filed his claim in 1994. Even though he had no history with Linux, nevertheless he was able to register a trademark in the USA. By 1996 a number of companies were trading successfully in Linux and Mr Della Croce stood to make a substantial amount of money!

With financial support from the Linux community, the vendor organisation Linux International fought and won the case in 1997. They demonstrated that many companies, themselves included, had been trading using the name Linux since 1992. Yet it didn't stop there – since that time there have been several attempts to file Linux as a trademark in other countries. An executive director of Linux International, Jon Hall (who usually calls himself 'maddog'), is quoted by the web magazine *Tux Deluxe* as saying:

> all around the world people were getting the same strange idea. [Free software advocates and developers] can't afford to go to the 200 countries around the world and buy trademarks, and maintain them, so we have to fight them on a case by case basis.

Quoted in Hillesley, 2007

Reputedly it costs about US$10 000 in lawyers' fees each time someone tries to file a claim for the Linux trademark. In 2007 this was estimated to have cost Linux International a total of US$300 000, most of which came from Jon 'maddog' Hall's personal wealth.

In 2005 maddog founded the Linux Mark Institute. Today, any company that trades using the name Linux is compelled to register with the institute and make a small donation in order to fund the protection of the trademark. The interesting thing about this compulsion is that, at least to some extent, it emerges because the trader wishes to protect their name rather than through pressure from the Linux community. That is to say, if a trader doesn't register with the institute then they risk someone else trying to register their trademark; on the other hand, if the trader chooses to register independently then they may find they are being sued by the Linux Mark Institute.

As you read in Section 1.2, the three ways in which intellectual property is protected are by patent, copyright and trademark. The copyright on Linux is protected by the GPL, but there was no similar mechanism for protecting Linux as a trademark. This is the sort of thing that a conventional business would have resolved from the outset.

Version control

When developing software, version control can present major difficulties. You might have found it necessary to keep several versions of a document when working on an assignment. Imagine what it would be like if there were several contributors all working on the same document – how would you know that you were contributing to the current version? To overcome difficulties like these, Linus Torvalds used a commercial version control package called BitKeeper, manufactured by a company called BitMover. Although the Linux developers, particularly Linus Torvalds, were allowed to use BitKeeper free of charge, not all members of the open source community were comfortable with using proprietary software. In particular, as you might imagine, Richard Stallman objected to using it.

Eventually, the Linux community were forced to go it alone and develop their own open source version control software, after an alleged BitKeeper licence violation led to the copyright holder, Larry McVoy, withdrawing the right for Linux developers to use it free of charge. The replacement was called Git – a rather unfortunate name from a UK perspective! It probably stood for Global Information Tracker, although I prefer Linus Torvalds' typically modest response when asked:

> I'm an egotistical b–tard, and I name all my projects after myself. First Linux, now git.

In fact Torvalds did do most of the early work on Git, but then the open source community took it over and developed it. Now Git is a widely used software version management tool and a good example of how the open source community is able to look after its own interests when pushed.

Political forces

An open source company is affected by wider political issues in the same way as any other. However, things like trade embargos run counter to everything the open source community stands for. The message below was posted to the 'Blog' section of the SourceForge website in 2010. The post clearly shows the dilemma in which SourceForge found itself in complying with US law. The fact that SourceForge is owned by a commercial company was probably a factor here too. The company's decision caused much dismay in open source circles.

Clarifying SourceForge.net's denial of site access for certain persons in accordance with US law

Posted on Monday, January 25th, 2010 by leeschlesinger

Category: General

If you follow @sourceforge on Twitter, you may have seen some tweets last week from certain users outside the US complaining that they no longer had access to SourceForge.net. Here's why.

Since 2003, the SourceForge.net Terms and Conditions of Use have prohibited certain persons from receiving services pursuant to U.S. laws, including, without limitations, the Denied Persons List and the Entity List, and other lists issued by the U.S. Department of

Commerce, Bureau of Industry and Security. The specific list of sanctions that affect our users concern the transfer and export of certain technology to foreign persons and governments on the sanctions list. This means users residing in countries on the United States Office of Foreign Assets Control (OFAC) sanction list, including Cuba, Iran, North Korea, Sudan, and Syria, may not post content to, or access content available through, SourceForge.net. Last week, SourceForge.net began automatic blocking of certain IP addresses to enforce those conditions of use.

As one of the first companies to promote the adoption and distribution of free and open source software, and one that still puts open source at the center of its corporate ideals, restrictions on the free flow of information rub us the wrong way. However, in addition to participating in the open source community, we also live in the real world, and are governed by the laws of the country in which we are located. Our need to follow those laws supersedes any wishes we might have to make our community as inclusive as possible. The possible penalties for violating these restrictions include fines and imprisonment. Other hosting companies based in the US have similar legal and technical restrictions in place.

We regret deeply that these sanctions may impact individuals who have no malicious intent along with those whom the rules are designed to punish. However, until either the designated governments alter the practices that got them on the sanctions list, or the US government's policies change, the situation must remain as it is.

Schlesinger, 2010

Activity 27 (self-assessment)

Summarise the blog post above in just a few sentences.

4.5   Conclusion

Understanding open source software development in the context of business models is challenging and ever changing. The main changes that seem to be taking place are in vertical development, where the move to cloud computing is being largely facilitated by open source software. Who could have predicted that companies such as IBM and Intel would find themselves collaborating to produce open source software? However, it doesn't stop there. In the final session I will go on to describe how the open source model is being developed beyond software.

This session should have helped you with the following learning outcomes.

- Explain how it is possible to develop business models from open source initiatives.
- Relate different business models that are based around open source.

5

Open source beyond software

The origins of the internet lie in the Request for Comments (RFC) process. Today RFCs are memoranda published by the Internet Engineering Task Force describing internet standards and protocols, but originally they were quite literally requests for comments on the development of the ARPANET from the network working group. The ARPANET grew into the internet and the rest, as they say, is history. The open nature of the architecture of the internet owes much to the RFC process and has been central to its success. For example, the open protocol of TCP/IP enabled anyone with the necessary skills to join in. I've chosen the ARPANET as an example here because it's not software that we're dealing with, but the open design of a communications network.

Similarly, you have read about how IBM designed its first personal computer to have what was referred to as *open architecture*. The idea of open architecture was that other companies could produce software and peripheral devices for the PC. IBM didn't do this out of any sense of altruism, but because it needed to sell PCs – and for PCs to sell there needed to be available software and other components, such as additional memory, which at the time IBM was not able to manufacture. Looking back, the impact of this was astonishing. A whole industry developed around the PC which, within a year, included clone machines that would also run the same software and use the same peripherals. Oddly, the clear winner in this environment turned out to be the software manufacturer Microsoft, whose MS-DOS operating system dominated the PC industry and who continued to dominate with Windows.

In this session I want to look at how the open source model has extended beyond software and even beyond computing.

5.1 It's good to share

In 1911, Henry Ford (the car manufacturer) and a small group of other car makers won a landmark patent dispute against George B. Seldon, who held the patent covering all petrol-powered vehicles. After the case Ford, along with several other manufacturers, established a group that eventually became the Motor Vehicle Manufacturers' Association. The members of this group all agreed to share their patents with the rest of the group.

Activity 28 (exploratory)

Why do you think individual manufacturers in the group agreed to share their patents with other group members?

Comment

The following quotation from *The Car Culture* by James Flink (1975) best sums up the position.

> Up to the outbreak of World War II, the Ford Motor Company permitted 92 of its patents to be used by others and in turn used 515 outside patents without any cash changing hands.

There was much more to gain by sharing.

This is really the key to the success of many open source products and at the time it was critical to the future of the US automobile industry. Of course, it's rather a simplistic answer, because not all patents are of equal value and the cost of companies paying each other for patents would have been passed on to the customer in the price of the product anyway. On the other hand, it was Henry Ford who, for better or worse, turned motoring from a hobby for the wealthy into a necessity for the masses, and he was able to do this because his products were cheap.

This form of patent sharing isn't open source as such, since the patents are only shared amongst a small group of stakeholders, but the principle of gaining through sharing and solving each other's problems is surely the same.

5.2 Creative Commons

The notion of information as property has been around for a very long time – that's why copyright and patents exist. The alternative to ownership is *commons*, which is a term that describes shared ownership for all. Think of a piece of common land: the land is free for all to use, nobody can assert ownership of it.

Creative Commons is an organisation that was established in 2001 with the stated aim of expanding the range of creative works available for others to build upon legally and to share. It has released several copyright licences that essentially allow people to choose the rights they pass on with their works. In many ways these are similar to the open source licences I discussed earlier, such as the GPL, but they apply to creative works. Creative Commons licences are used to cover many things including pieces of writing, ideas, films, images and designs. They allow reuse of material in the same way that the GPL allows people to copy and pass on software.

Some Creative Commons licences are quite restrictive – for example, they refuse the right to produce derivative works. This has led to criticism from people such as Richard Stallman, who see such activities as being essential.

Third-party material

As with software, 'giving it all away' isn't always easy. Recently a consortium was established to provide archive film and TV materials for release under a Creative Commons licence. The consortium consisted of many organisations that possess this type of material, such as the BBC, Channel 4, the British Film Institute, ITN and even The Open University. Yet this turns out to be a very complex thing to attempt to do, because most film material contains things that have their own copyrights.

The BBC is funded by the UK licence payer, which means that it has an obligation to the UK but not to the rest of the world. This creates a rather awkward situation because Creative Commons licences are not generally constrained by national boundaries. The BBC often only owns the right to broadcast the material, not the material itself.

Take music, for example. A piece of music might belong to a record company that licenses it to be used in a particular film. Releasing this material under a Creative Commons licence requires that the music be released too. But the owners of the film might not have the right to do this; they only have the right to show the film with that music in it, not to release it for others to use. This applies to images, too; for example, a film might contain copyright images such as Mickey Mouse (Box 5), for which permission would have to have been sought.

Material like this is referred to as *third-party material*. Essentially this means it belongs to someone else and has usually only been cleared for use in a particular context.

> ### Box 5 Mickey Mouse
>
> Mickey Mouse is trademarked and copyrighted by Walt Disney Co. Recently a dispute arose over whether or not Disney owns all the versions of Mickey Mouse, because Mickey appears in an early cartoon called 'Steamboat Willie'. In this cartoon he has longer arms, a more pointed nose and smaller ears. The copyright on the Mickey Mouse in 'Steamboat Willie' may have allowed a loophole that could mean that this particular version of Mickey is not owned by Disney.
>
> What is interesting here is that there is room for judgement in these things. How small do the ears have to be before it's no longer Mickey Mouse?

Delivering learning

There are several examples of organisations 'open sourcing' their products. For instance, The Open University does this with some study materials through OpenLearn. This was done with support from the

Hewlett Foundation, a philanthropic organisation committed to various goals that include improving educational provision.

Activity 29 (exploratory)

In this activity you will visit OpenLearn and look at the copyright notice on some of the material. When convenient, go to the resources page associated with this part on the TU100 website and follow the instructions there.

Again the process of sharing materials is a far from straightforward proposition, because it is not possible simply to take OU copyright material such as TU100 and distribute it under a Creative Commons licence. Similar to the problems encountered with film and TV, OU modules contain a lot of third-party material that has to be either cleared for release or removed.

Hardware

The open source model has also found its way into the world of hardware. For instance, your SenseBoard uses an Arduino interface whose design is licensed under a Creative Commons licence. This confers a very similar entitlement to an open source licence agreement, in that it entitles the user to alter the design provided that they pass on the altered design. It is possible to embed an Arduino in a proprietary product without being compelled to open source the rest of the design, but any alterations to the Arduino design would have to be passed on.

5.3   Rivalrous and non-rivalrous commodities

What I hope you are beginning to see is that the things that are best adapted to open source are in the form of intellectual property. Economists use two terms to describe different commodities that may help you to understand this: *rivalrous* and *non-rivalrous*. Put simply, a rivalrous commodity is something that cannot be taken without depriving the owner of it. For example, a car is rivalrous – if somebody else takes my car I am deprived of it. However, in the case of a non-rivalrous commodity I am not deprived of the commodity; so, for example, if someone takes one of my ideas then I still possess the idea. This is also true for things such as music and films that can be easily duplicated. It is the non-rivalrous commodities that are most easily developed as open source products.

Activity 30 (exploratory)

Below is a list of activities. Which ones lend themselves to being open sourced or produced under a Creative Commons licence? You might like to start by considering which have rivalrous and which non-rivalrous products at their heart. You could also refer back to Figure 11 at the end of Session 3 to see if you can identify the nature of the various entities involved and check the viability of your thinking.

Making a film

Designing a car

Manufacturing a car

Creating a computer game

Producing an electronic magazine or newspaper

Creating a book

Building a house

Comment

A lot of film material is released under a Creative Commons licence, so making a film should be perfectly possible. Duplication of a film for use on DVD or the Web is very easy, so in this sense it is a non-rivalrous product. In terms of Figure 11, there could be individuals supplying footage to a common product development area. Groups or individuals could identify appropriate footage, and creative artists and organisations could use this material to generate income.

Designing a car via open source could be possible – I will say more about this in Section 5.4 – and the design is certainly non-rivalrous. However, manufacturing things that require sophisticated tooling, etc. is going to be difficult. Referring to Figure 11, the designers could feed ideas to a common development area; however, there is much trial and error in car design and it's hard to see how such a community might share the necessary physical/prototype models.

There exist many open source computer games, and computer games can all be non-rivalrous products. In terms of Figure 11, this is certainly possible because it is software, so the model discussed for Linux is completely appropriate.

Many magazines on the Web contain material that is authored under a Creative Commons licence, and a website is certainly non-rivalrous. Referring to Figure 11, it is possible to envisage individuals submitting articles to a product development area and an editor acting to control quality and release versions of the articles that could be taken by vendors for publication.

Several books have been released under Creative Commons licences. There are even derivative works in some cases. If the book is released as an ebook then it too could be non-rivalrous.

It might be possible to open source the design of a house, but the construction would be too expensive.

5.4 Open source car

I started this session by talking about the car industry and patent sharing, so it seems appropriate to close by returning to this industry. It is probably the dominant manufacturing activity for many countries and operates on an international scale. Is there such a thing as an open source car?

There have certainly been many attempts and claims: OSCar, Local Car and Riversimple, to name but a few. However, at the time of writing it's hard to identify any major successes. Current models tend to be based on either open sourcing the design process or designing a car then open sourcing the design.

OSCar (Figure 15) was established in 1999 but appears to have 'stalled' in around 2006. OSCar did appear to be a genuine approach, in that it tried to open source the design process, but sadly a car never emerged. Interestingly, in the case of Riversimple a car did emerge but the process appears, to date, to have been closed source.

Figure 15 One conceptual design for OSCar

Activity 31 (exploratory)

Links to information on the Riversimple car, as well as some interesting open source developments in other contexts, are provided in the resources page associated with this part on the TU100 website. When you have finished reading this part you should go and explore these, but don't spend too long on this.

5.5 Conclusion

In this session you have seen how patent sharing and Creative Commons licences can be used to extend some of the principles of open source to all kinds of products beyond software. Ideas are non-rivalrous commodities and therefore lend themselves to the open source model, since you can allow other people to use your idea without losing it yourself – although, of course, you can't make money from just the idea if it's free to use.

This session should have helped you with the following learning outcome.

- Identify where it may be possible to extend open source methods.

Summary

When it comes to software, the open source movement appears to have been a remarkable success. Linux and other open source software products continue to go from strength to strength, and large businesses depend on the continued existence of such products.

It's less clear how projects beyond software, in the creative commons for example, will perform in the future. Existing products, such as digital media like film and TV, for the most part appear to be trapped in a mire of third-party rights. The non-rivalrous elements of products such as computer models and software designs have the potential to succeed, but it is hard to see which if any will.

Activity 32 (exploratory)

You are now halfway through your study of TU100, so this is the perfect point at which to return to the 'How digital is your life?' quiz that you carried out at the beginning of Block 1. Remember, there are no right or wrong answers to this quiz, but taking it again should help you to gauge how various aspects of your digital life have changed since your studies began.

If you can access the TU100 website at this moment, please go to the 'Study resources' section and work through the quiz for the second time. It doesn't matter if you can't attempt it straight away, but please try to do it soon.

Comment

Hopefully you found that your responses to many of the questions had changed as a result of learning about new ideas, developing new skills and becoming more confident in your digital life.

You have now completed your study of Block 3. Once you are satisfied that you have looked at all the resources associated with this part on the TU100 website, you can move on to Block 4, which broadens the focus of your study once more to look at the social aspects of a digital life: communicating, sharing and playing online. Part 1 of Block 4 is presented online, so you should now go to the TU100 website and start work on it.

Answers to self-assessment activities

Activity 3

1   You would be prevented on a practical level because you only have access to the machine code, and this is difficult to read and therefore modify.

2   In addition, in modifying the program you would probably be in breach of the licence agreement, which usually grants a user the right to use the code but not to modify it.

Activity 5

They can all be copyrighted.

Activity 7

The text was produced in the course of my employment with The Open University. Under those circumstances, the rules of copyright dictate that the copyright belongs to my employer.

Activity 8

Yes, it is. Whilst Dickens' original work is no longer under copyright and can be performed by anyone, the BBC adaptation of *Bleak House* is still protected by copyright. In the UK, the recording is protected for 50 years from the date of the first broadcast – that is, until 2056.

Activity 11

The licence agreement gives the end user permission (with certain restrictions) to use the product.

Activity 12

Studying how a program works and modifying it require access to the source code, so freedom 1 and freedom 3. The source code isn't required to run or distribute a straight copy of a program.

Activity 13

This really depends on how you define success, an issue that I deliberately left open in the question. It could be that you define it in terms of popularity, trustworthiness, durability or sustainability. All of these are legitimate ways of defining success, depending on your perspective.

Given this, there are probably many reasons, but to me the most significant are:

*   the motivation and energy of its creators (primarily Stallman and Torvalds) – leading to success in terms of durability and sustainability

- its reliability (owing to the vast developer community) – popularity, trustworthiness, durability
- its low cost (it has a free licence) – popularity.

Activity 15

(a) Recorded usage share is the number of requests for pages made by a particular type of browser.

(b) There are many reasons why the figure might not be an accurate representation of the market share, but the main source of inaccuracy is that it is a measure of which browsers are requesting information and not of how many users are using a particular browser. Also, the browsing habits of users differ according to their level of experience.

Activity 18

I've mentioned physical models, mathematical models, computer models and diagrammatic models.

Activity 20

There are four elements in the definition of a *system*:

1 it should consist of an *assembly* of components that *interact*
2 the components are *affected* if they are removed from or *enter* the assembly
3 the assembly should have a *purpose*
4 the assembly should have been identified as being of interest to a *human*.

Activity 22

The roles might be as follows.

- The contributors would be the authors of the material, sending entries into the product development area.
- The product development area would be an open area on the internet where developers could alter and suggest materials.
- The quality control could be a group of individuals or an organisation that ensures the entries are correct.
- The vendors could be publishers who add value by selling the materials as books, providing search services via the Web, etc.

I am sure your answer looked different from mine, but I hope you can see that we have the basis of a model for beginning to understand open source activities in general.

Activity 24

This method of working presents a problem for software that is based on open source code, since all derivatives of the code also have to be open source.

Activity 26

The dual licensing model allows a business to license *proprietary* software that contains open source code.

Consulting companies rely on charging for advising companies on *open source* software and helping to customise it.

Companies can package software and add value by including *support* and installation instructions.

Vertical development of hybrid proprietary/open source software enables companies to support activities such as *cloud* computing.

Companies that collaborate with each other and the *developer* community to produce open source software are said to be working horizontally.

Activity 27

Cuba, Iran, North Korea, Sudan and Syria are on a US government sanctions list. As such, the owners of SourceForge risk fines or imprisonment if they allow people in these countries access to their services. The owners are uncomfortable with the situation, because it cuts across open source values, but feel they have no choice.

Glossary

American Telephone and Telegraph (AT&T)   A vast US telecommunications company.

commons   Something that is collectively shared by every human being.

copyleft   An alternative to copyright that uses copyright law to pass on the rights to alter and distribute derivatives of a work that is copyleft protected.

copyright   A legal protection that guarantees that creators of content are rewarded for their work and protects the rights of users.

Creative Commons licence   A licence permitting the copying, distribution, display and performance of work.

domain   A named collection of hosts on the internet. Some domains, such as .uk, are geographically based; others, such as .com, are not.

dotcom boom   A period from the mid-1990s to around the year 2000 when frenzied investment took place in internet-based companies.

end-user licence agreement (EULA)   A legal contract between the software's copyright owner and the user that details the circumstances in which the software may be used.

general public licence (GPL)   A licence that grants the user freedom to run, redistribute and modify software.

input–output (IO) driver   Software that provides the interface between a computer and its peripherals.

intellectual property rights (IPR)   The law relating to ownership of ideas, writing and other works of the mind.

kernel   A program that forms the inner core of an operating system.

Linux production kernel   The most important part of the Linux operating system, which has to be totally reliable.

machine language   A very low-level, symbolic representation of instructions at the level of the instruction set of a CPU, usually using a binary numeric representation. Also known as *machine code*.

model   A simplified representation of something, constructed for a specific purpose.

open source   Originally, software provided with source code.

patch   A temporary fix to a bug or security problem in a particular piece of software (such as a web browser or an operating system). A patch modifies existing software rather than replacing it with a new version.

patent A form of protection that gives the creator of a piece of work exclusive rights to use, produce and sell the work for a limited period of time in exchange for the creator making public the design and workings of the item.

public domain A term referring to any created content that is not subject to copyright. Material that is 'in the public domain' may be used freely by anyone.

recursive acronym An abbreviation that refers to itself – very common in software titles. For instance, in the case of GNU the letter G stands for GNU.

rights Entitlements of a legal nature.

source code Text representing a program that is usually input into a compiler or interpreter. Source code is usually written in a high-level language, but can be written in low-level and assembler languages. Also known as a *source program*.

synergy A process in which two or more components of a system interact to create an overall effect that is different from that of the individual components.

total cost of ownership The cost of a product, including not only the purchase price but also indirect costs such as training of staff in its use and implementation costs.

trademark A particular word or phrase and/or artwork that distinguishes a company's goods and services.

typographical arrangement The layout of text, images and pictures in a published work.

Unix An operating system that was popular in the 1980s and is still widely used today.

vendor lock-in A situation where the customer is dependent on a vendor for products and services and is unable to switch to an alternative supplier without incurring substantial costs.

webmaster A highly skilled technician who develops and maintains web resources.

References

Deek, F.P. and McHugh, J.A.M. (2007) *Open Source: Technology and Policy*, New York, Cambridge University Press.

Fildes, J. (2010) 'Symbian phone operating system goes open source', *BBC News* [online], 4 February, http://news.bbc.co.uk/1/hi/technology/8496263.stm (accessed 22 October 2010).

Flink, J.J. (1975) *The Car Culture*, Cambridge, MA, MIT Press.

Free Software Foundation (2010) *The Free Software Definition* (version 1.92) [online], Free Software Foundation, Inc., http://www.gnu.org/philosophy/free-sw.html (accessed 22 October 2010).

Hillesley, R. (2007) 'Asterix, the Gall – The Strange History of Linux and Trademarks', *Tux Deluxe* [online], 27 March, http://tuxdeluxe.org/node/107 (accessed 22 October 2010).

Leonard, A. (1998) 'The saint of free software', *Salon* [online], 30 July, http://www.salon.com/technology/feature/1998/07/30/feature (accessed 22 October 2010).

Raymond, E.S. (1999) *The Cathedral & The Bazaar: Musings on Linux and Open Source by an Accidental Revolutionary*, Sebastopol, CA, O'Reilly Media; also available online at http://catb.org/esr/writings/cathedral-bazaar/ (accessed 22 October 2010).

Schlesinger, L. (2010) 'Clarifying SourceForge.net's denial of site access for certain persons in accordance with US law', message posted on SourceForge blog, 25 January.

Schneider, J. (2003) 'Interview: PHP Founder Rasmus Lerdorf on Relinquishing Control', *ePrairie* [online], April, http//www.midwestbusiness.com/printer/article.asp?newsletterID=4577 (accessed 1 March 2010).

Stallman, R. (1985) *The GNU Manifesto* [online], Free Software Foundation, Inc., http://www.gnu.org/gnu/manifesto.html (accessed 22 October 2010).

Tanenbaum, A. (1992) 'Re: LINUX is obsolete', message posted on Usenet, 30 January.

Torvalds, L. (1991a) 'What would you like to see most in minix?', message posted on Usenet, 25 August.

Torvalds, L. (1991b) 'Free minix-like kernel sources for 386-AT', message posted on Usenet, 5 October.

Acknowledgements

Grateful acknowledgement is made to the following sources.

Text
Quotation pp. 109–10: From www.gnu.org

Quotations pp. 111–12 and 112–13: Courtesy of Ragib Hasan

Quotation pp. 143–4: Taken from http://sourceforge.net/Lee Schlesinger

Figures
Figure 4: © Chris McKenna; taken from www.wikipedia.org and used under Creative Commons Licence, http://creativecommons.org/licenses/by-sa/3.0/deed.en

Figure 15: Courtesy of The Oscar Project